New

Voices

in

American

Studies

New Voices in American Studies

Edited by

Ray B. Browne

Donald M. Winkelman

and

Allen Hayman

1966   Purdue University Studies

To Paul Fatout
Scholar and Friend

Contents

LITERATURE

Literature and American Studies: Some New Directions..... 11
    Allen Hayman

American Radicals and Literary Works of the Mid-nineteenth
Century 13
    Leo Stoller

Mark Twain and the Upward Mobility of Taste............ 21
    Louis J. Budd

A Tale of Two Authors: Theodore Dreiser and David Graham
Phillips 35
    Louis Filler

John Hersey: War Correspondent into Novelist............ 49
    David Sanders

"The Strenuous Life" as a Theme in American Cultural History 59
    Edwin H. Cady

The Juvenile Approach to American Culture, 1870-1930...... 67
    Russel B. Nye

POPULAR CULTURE, FOLKLORE, AND ETHNOMUSICOLOGY

Catalysts for Interdisciplinary Study..................... 87
    Donald M. Winkelman

Popular Theater in *Moby Dick*.......................... 89
    Ray R. Browne

Real Use and Real Abuse of Folklore in the Writer's Subconscious: F. Scott Fitzgerald.......................... 102
    Tristram P. Coffin

The Anglo-American in Mexican Folklore.................. 113
    Américo Paredes

Some Influences of Western Civilization on North American
Indian Music 129
    Bruno Nettl

The Origin and Tradition of the Ballad of "Thomas Rhymer" 138
    C. E. Nelson

Some Rhythmic Aspects of the Child Ballad................ 151
    Donald M. Winkelman

A Note on Contributors.................................. 163

Introduction:

The Proper Study for American Studies

Through the years the various scholarly fields loosely associated with "American Studies" have developed into a coherent discipline with momentum. This discipline has made a determined effort to achieve comprehensiveness, to cover all aspects of American culture (or cultures). For an even longer period, scholars in American folklore have grown in number and in seriousness about their subject. Unfortunately for both disciplines, there has been little association between the two.

But new thinking, new energies, new movements are at work. Revised logic in American Studies urges that the isolated regional chapters grow into larger, more productive loose federations. Scholars in this discipline are recognizing that much is to be gained from (relative) bigness, from the larger communities in which people who are interested in the same fields or related areas get to know one another personally and professionally.

American folklore is also experiencing a new burst of energy in areas which in the past were comparatively slighted—such as material culture, folk arts and crafts, folk literature, and folklore in literature. Increasingly, scholars in folklore are cooperating with those in related fields, for example, in ethnomusicology.

The time has come when serious scholars in these various disciplines—American Studies, folklore, and others—should realize the nature of one another's work and the potential value and need each field has for the others. To be comprehensive, American Studies, that is, the examination of American life and culture, must include subculture—folk and popular cultures—as well: Sut Lovingood as well as Herman Melville, the teller of the Alabama folktale as well as the greater and more serious artist from Missouri, Mark Twain; the folk aesthetic as well as the more sophis-

7

ticated one. Folklore, also, to be as strong and significant as it should be must chin itself on the cultures above it.

The Mid-America Conference on Literature, History, Popular Culture and Folklore held at Purdue University in the spring of 1965 was organized to demonstrate the need for closer alliance among the disciplines. The papers in this volume, all but two of which were read at that Conference, illustrate the logic of the combination. They speak emphatically and conclusively to the point that in the various fields and levels of American Studies and folklore, a broader and more liberal approach would be a more proper study.

Ray B. Browne

Literature

Literature and American Studies:
Some New Directions

Allen Hayman

Most of the papers grouped here somewhat loosely under the heading of "literature" illustrate precisely what the organizers of the Mid-America Conference on Literature, History, Popular Culture, and Folklore hoped they would: that these various disciplines are inter-related and necessary one to the other. There is nothing parochial about most of these papers, and that is much of their value. They illustrate fruitful areas and approaches that other scholars in American Studies might explore. Had the writers of most of these papers restricted themselves rigidly to exclusively "literary" studies we readers would have been deprived of the richness that has been derived from their ranging widely over their subjects, even when it meant exploring areas not generally considered literary or strictly within the province of American Studies. They are all, however, concerned in the broadest sense with various aspects of American culture.

Thus, Russel Nye's exploration of essentially subliterary material has provided us with a deeper insight into the American experience of the late nineteenth and early twentieth centuries—and has led the way for other scholars to follow. The uses to which journalistic techniques have been put by the novelist John Hersey are succinctly indicated by David Sanders, and Leo Stoller has yoked such disparate entities as the writings in a vegetarian magazine of 1843 and literary work by Hawthorne, Melville, and Thoreau—suggesting how they illuminate each other. Louis Filler has suggested that an examination of the life as well as the work of two early twentieth-century novelists—one mainly obscured by time, the other still read and discussed—can contribute to our

11

awareness of American culture. Louis J. Budd has explored Mark Twain's "career" as a viewer and "appreciator" of painting and sculpure—and has shown how Twain's unsure taste in painting is reflected in his own literary work and his judgment (or misjudgment) of that work. Each of these scholars has approached his literary figures through what is mainly nonliterary material, and each has demonstrated how these materials enrich our understanding of the literature. Edwin H. Cady, the final writer represented here, has eschewed "literature" entirely in his paper but has pointed to material that others (and hopefully Mr. Cady himself) will examine for a more complete understanding of many of our literary writers. As these scholars intended, their papers give us a greater knowledge of both American literature and American culture. We all can benefit from these new directions.

American Radicals and Literary Works of the Mid-nineteenth Century: An Analogy

Leo Stoller

I want to suggest an analogy between a few American radicals of the mid-nineteenth century and a few American literary works of the same period. I can illustrate it most quickly with two quotations.

The first is from an anonymous author writing in a vegetarian magazine whose only issue appeared in 1843. He has been telling artists and intellectuals that they will work better on less food and less sex—or, as he puts it, on "the smallest supply of physical food and the holiest desire of soul." Then he chooses to reply to a criticism of his thesis, and it is his paraphrase of the criticism that I call to your attention. "Literary men make for themselves a sad mistake," he cautions, "when they range the subject of diet on a level with dandyism in dress, or dilettantism in art: when they assure us that unleavened bread and an unshaven chin are alike the results of perverted universal ideas taking refuge in a corner, *they can rule,* from the common-sense world which has ruled and repelled them."[1]

The second is from Ishmael's explanation of why Captain Ahab is hunting Moby Dick. He has just told us how Ahab lost his leg to the White Whale, and he goes on as follows:

> Small reason was there to doubt, then, that ever since that almost fatal encounter, Ahab had cherished a wild vindictiveness against the whale, all the more fell for that in his frantic morbidness he at last came to identify with him, not only all his bodily woes, but all his intellectual and spiritual exasperations. . . . That intangible malignity which has been from the beginning . . . Ahab did not fall down and worship it

> . . . but deliriously transferring its idea to the abhorred white whale, he pitted himself, all mutilated, against it. All that most maddens and torments; all that stirs up the lees of things; all truth with malice in it; all that cracks the sinews and cakes the brain; all the subtle demonisms of life and thought; all evil, to craze Ahab, were visibly personified, and made practically assailable in Moby Dick.[2]

Now to point an analogy with Ahab is to speak of the great extreme. We shall occasionally find a reformer who is so much an "ultraist" (to use one label of that day) that he makes a single act the precondition for all adequate social change. Thus a vegetarian in the same magazine I quoted from a moment ago writes: "so incalculably potent is the influence of bodily health on the intellectual and moral state, that without soundness here all hope for Humanity is dim indeed." This man's heart aches "for that huge majority of our kind, to whom Life is so dreary a thing, smothered by ignorance, goaded by grim famine to hard, incessant unattractive toil, incrusted with squalor and meanness." He will not "strike truce with a Social Order" that breeds every kind of slavery. But first he would have us all switch from meat to vegetables.[3] The fictional monomaniac embodies all evil in a White Whale that can be tracked and lowered for. The ultraist lays siege to evil in the kitchen, where it can be starved out through Physiological Reform. But Ahab is nearly unique in our fiction, and social fetishists like this vegetarian are not a commonplace of nineteenth-century reality. Each is best thought of as a limit that other characters and other people come near but do not actually reach.

If we look for American men and women who approached the limit of social fetishism, we shall find them most easily among the abolitionists who attended the Peace Convention in Boston's Marlboro Chapel in 1838 and agreed to its "Declaration of Sentiments."[4] These people chose to control their action in "the common-sense world" by a set of restrictive principles that they named "Non-Resistance." They recognized only "one king and law giver, one judge and ruler of mankind." Therefore they could not support any human government, which was invariably ungodlike, they could not hold office, they could not campaign in politics, they could not vote. They felt themselves "bound by the laws of a kingdom which is not of this world; the subjects of which are forbidden to fight." Therefore they could never use violence or put anyone else in a position that invited violence, could not bear arms, could not undertake lawsuits, could not hit back and

punish but had to forgive and submit. To this common catalog, many of them added still other prohibitions. Almost all abstained from coffee, tea, and meat. Some even abstained from organizations.

All of these people, however, were abolitionists. As the years brought the founding of the Liberty Party, the passage of the Fugitive Slave Law, the trial war in Kansas, the attack on Harper's Ferry, and ultimately the Second American Revolution, each of them was forced to choose between the pragmatic demands of the campaign to free the slaves and the higher-law injunctions of nonresistance. Here physiological reform posed no problem. Two men could eat sparingly together at the Grahamite inn even though one had just spoken for organized action and the other for spontaneity. But between 1840 and 1861 every nonresistant had to make a choice between organization and no-organization, between violence and nonviolence, between politics and no-politics.

It was a time of separating paths for them, and their beliefs were repeatedly being called into question. If man refused to vote when the Liberty Party ran candidates, he had to make his choice again with the Free Soil Party or the Republican Party. If he refused to approve violence to free Anthony Burns, he might change his mind when John Brown fought in Kansas or in Virginia or when the first shots were exchanged at Fort Sumter. In the end only Adin Ballou and a handful of others were still defending their original doctrine. But the Garrisons and Alcotts and Wrights did not give up nonresistance all at once. They tended to abandon it piece by piece, and at the moment of choice they wrote as if all good and all evil were represented in the two tactics at issue.

The impulse whose limit is social fetishism can also be found outside physiological reform and nonresistance and outside the perfectionism of which these are particular instances. But here it is more difficult to abstract and to present in simple paradigm. I shall therefore give only the most obvious example: the compulsion to live in the commonwealth of small producers while the rest of nonslaveholding America was moving into industrial capitalism.

Orestes Brownson stated the argument in his 1840 essay "The Laboring Classes." His premise was this: "The great evil of all modern society, in relation to the material order, is the separation of the capitalist from the labourer,—the division of the community into two classes, one of which owns the funds, and the other of which performs the labor of production." And among his conclusions were these: first, that "there must be no class of our fellow men doomed to toil through life as mere workmen at wages"; second, that we must "combine labour and capital in the same individual."[5]

Brownson's argument might well be a gloss to Thoreau's chapter on "Economy," to Alcott's letters about Fruitlands, and to other utopian manifestos. The come-outers who set up arcadian economies outside the main drift of America's livelihood considered themselves reformers of society rather than of the individual. They did not stop with the body, as did the physiologists. Or with slavery, as did the Garrisonian nonresistants. They went on to the machine and the market. But they confronted them outside "the common-sense world," in a specially created environment where they meant to exercise total control over their occupations, their politics and their personalities. The conflict within a utopian who had withdrawn from the world he grew up in was therefore more complex than that in a man who sat in his Boston grocery making up his mind about going to the polls. It involved much more of his life and might break out where least expected, the center of his psyche lying perhaps on the periphery of his ideology. Thoreau's, for example, shows up in "Higher Laws" in terms of the flesh, not the economy. But the conflict was always there, and in the end nearly every man who went to Walden found his way back to Concord.

If we return now to the literary side of my analogy, we see that Ahab is not enough. We must bring in Ishmael as well. Ahab has observed destruction and injustice all his life and has become obsessed by his inability to find the source at which they can be attacked. When Moby Dick rips off his leg, he becomes more than ever aware of his impotence. He then incarnates the general evil of the world in this particular White Whale, transferring it from a region beyond his control to one where he considers himself master. The process by which inadequate, ideological thought turns into fetishism is here fully represented. Ahab then pursues Moby Dick, stubbornly, heroically, and acts out the tragedy potential in this process.

Ishmael goes only part of the way. He too is driven to do something about that "damp, drizzly November" in the soul. He too thinks the White Whale will yield an answer or, what may be worse, reveal that there is no answer. But in a series of chapters climaxed by "The Try-Works" (which is immediately preceded by the celebration of "The Cassock"), Ishmael abandons Ahab's extremism. When he narrates the events some years later, he is a different man. He loves the world and cannot have enough of it, but he no longer tries to drive life into a corner.

Melville's characterization of Ahab through the mouth of Ishmael is closely paralleled by Hawthorne's characterization of Hollingsworth through the mouth of Coverdale. When Coverdale is ill and being nursed by Hollingsworth in the farmhouse of the Blithedale utopia, the two young men talk about Fourier, and Hollingsworth's rage at the great socialist reveals the true state of his mind to the narrator.

"I began to discern," writes Coverdale, "that he had come among us actuated by no real sympathy with our feelings and our hopes, but chiefly because we were estranging ourselves from the world, with which his lonely and exclusive object in life had already put him at odds." This exclusive object was a new institution for the reform of criminals. To it went all of Hollingsworth's "great spirit of benevolence." When you needed him he could be "the tenderest man and the truest friend on earth." But soon you saw that his mind had turned inward to brood on his scheme. "This was a result exceedingly sad to contemplate," continues Coverdale,

> considering that it had been mainly brought about by the very ardor and exuberance of his philanthropy. Sad, indeed, but by no means unusual: he had taught his benevolence to pour its warm tide exclusively through one channel; so that there was nothing to spare for other great manifestations of love to man, nor scarcely for the nutriment of individual attachments, unless they could minister, in some way, to the terrible egotism which he mistook for an angel of God. Had Hollingsworth's education been more enlarged, he might not so inevitably have stumbled into this pitfall. But this identical pursuit had educated him. He knew absolutely nothing, except in a single direction, where he had thought so energetically, and felt to such a depth, that, no doubt, the entire reason and justice of the universe appeared to be concentrated thitherward.

It was not enough for Hollingsworth to absorb all goodness into a single abstraction. He was forever sketching the rooms of the model prison or building them out of pebbles, so that Coverdale remarks:

> His visionary edifice was Hollingsworth's one castle in the air; it was the material type in which his philanthropic dream strove to embody itself; and he made the scheme more definite, and caught hold of it

the more strongly, and kept his clutch the more pertinaciously, by rendering it visible to the bodily eye.[6]

Thoreau tells us at the end of *Walden* that "if you have built castles in the air, your work need not be lost"—you have only to "put the foundations under them." But he does not say that on his way out to the pond, he says it on his way back to the world. To anchor your dreams in a single element abstracted from the rest of reality is to run the risk of Hollingsworth and Ahab. To found them on reality is to turn back with Ishmael and with Thoreau.

It is with the instant of discovery, the point of turning back, that I wish to end this brief exploration of my analogy. I have already mentioned two such moments, in "The Try-Works" and in "Higher Laws." I stumbled on a third a number of years ago, in Thoreau's essay "Katahdin"[7] and have since noticed two parallels to it.

Thoreau climbed Katahdin hoping to sense the union of matter and spirit, as he had on previous excursions to hilltops. Above the treeline he discovered that instead of finding his soul he was losing it. "Some part of the beholder, even some vital part," he wrote, "seems to escape through the loose grating of his ribs as he ascends." In place of spirit there was only "Matter, vast, terrific." Thoreau's reaction to this disappointment is best caught from his own words:

> What is it to be admitted to a museum, to see a myriad of particular things, compared with being shown some star's surface, some hard matter in its home! I stand in awe of my body, this matter to which I am bound has become so strange to me. I fear not spirits, ghosts, of which I am one,—*that* my body might,—but I fear bodies, I tremble to meet them. What is this Titan that has possession of me? Talk of mysteries! Think of our life in nature,—daily to be shown matter, to come in contact with it,—rocks, trees, wind on our cheeks! the *solid* earth! the *actual* world! the *common sense*! *Contact! Contact! Who* are we? *where* are we?

Some of the terror of this passage is owing to Thoreau's loss of nature as Mother, linking it to the moment of discovery in "Higher Laws." But the central fact is that he looked for mysticism and found only its opposite.

Observe now the narrator of *Moby Dick* looking back humorously on how he kept the lookout for whales from the masthead of the *Pequod*. There may have been "shoals of them in the far horizon," but Ishmael was one of those "young Platonists" who could not see the fins for the symbols. Above ship and ocean and earth he would fall into a mystical revery, and his older skeptical self addresses him in this state:

> There is no life in thee, now, except that rocking life imparted by a gently rolling ship; by her, borrowed from the sea; by the sea, from the inscrutable tides of God. But while this sleep, this dream is on ye, move your foot or hand an inch; slip your hold at all; and your identity comes back in horror. Over Descartian vortices you hover. And perhaps, at mid-day, in the fairest weather, with one half-throttled shriek you drop through that transparent air into the summer sea, no more to rise for ever. Heed it well, ye Pantheists![8]

Hawthorne uses this masthead image in a fascinating way in *The Marble Faun*.[9] You will recall that Hilda lives in the top story of a medieval tower and keeps a flame burning before an image of the Virgin. About this double shrine there is always a flock of white doves. One day she is visited by Miriam, who playfully takes Hilda at face value. "You breathe sweet air," she tells her, "above all the evil scents of Rome; and even so, in your maiden elevation, you dwell above our vanities and passions, our moral dust and mud, with the doves and the angels for your nearest neighbors." But Hilda really does believe in this false image of herself. "The air so exhilarates my spirits," she says, "that sometimes I feel half inclined to attempt a flight from the top of my tower, in the faith that I should float upward." And upon hearing this remark, her slightly older and much more experienced friend pulls her up short: "If it should turn out that you are less than an angel, you would find the stones of the Roman pavement very hard; and if an angel, indeed, I am afraid you would never come down among us again."

In the passage by Thoreau we see an actual utopian experimenter at the moment when one element of the ideology that took him to Walden Pond suddenly failed to correspond to his reality. The passage from Melville is a fictional representation of an almost identical experience, told by a character who has already learned that the world will persist in being itself and that the shock of reality is greatest for the man who has withdrawn from it the furthest. In the selection from Hawthorne, the conflict between ideology and reality touches on the distortion that can be introduced ito the psyche through stubborn adherence to high notions of self-denial. Whether it would be wise to suggest that next to these three stands Pierre and next to him Billy Budd, I have not yet decided. The danger with an analogy is always the danger of exaggeration.

Notes

1. "Literature and Diet," *The Health Journal and Independent Magazine: Devoted to Universal Christian Philosophy,* I (February 1843), 22 f. His italics.

2. Herman Melville, *Moby Dick, or The Whale,* ed. Luther S. Mansfield and Howard P. Vincent (New York, 1952), 181.

3. D.H.B., "The Times," *The Health Journal and Independent Magazine,* I (February 1843), 12 f.

4. *Proceedings of the Peace Convention Held in Boston, in the Marlboro Chapel, September 18, 19, & 20, 1838,* Boston, 1838.

5. *Boston Quarterly Review,* III (July 1840), 373; (October 1840), 467, 472.

6. *The Works of Nathaniel Hawthorne,* Standard Library Edition, 15 vols., (Boston and New York, n.d.), V, 381-83.

7. *After Walden: Thoreau's Changing Views on Economic Man* (Stanford, 1957), 45-47.

8. *Moby Dick,* ed. Mansfield and Vincent, 156 f.

9. *The Works of Nathaniel Hawthorne,* VI, 70 f.

Mark Twain and The Upward Mobility of Taste

Louis J. Budd

As Henry James's first mature novel *The American* (1877) begins, Christopher Newman, self-reliant westerner and self-made man, is in the Museum of the Louvre, staring wearily at a famous canvas but feeling "profound enjoyment" in his stance. No matter how fatigued by his "tranquil stroll" through the Louvre, he now enjoys the sense of upgrading himself. But his triumph is shaky. Raphael, Titian, and Rubens—says James—"inspired our friend, for the first time in his life, with a vague self-mistrust." Even so, he does not feel enough self-mistrust to keep from "often" admiring the "copy much more than the original." Before our eyes, in fact, he directs his admiration toward a young copyist and contracts to buy her work. Later he contracts for six more copies, unwittingly choosing, she tells him, the six most difficult paintings in the Louvre. Besides, as she confesses, she has no talent as a copyist, a verdict confirmed in one glance by a gay blade of a French aristocrat.

Only James, of the major American novelists of his time, could have created this interplay. William Dean Howells never dared to claim such certainty of taste in painting; Stephen Crane had a sensitive and confident eye but despised any pretensions to elevated taste; and Mark Twain came painfully close to being Newman at the Louvre. Ten months before the date of the opening action in *The American*, Twain had arrived in Paris as the traveling correspondent for a California newspaper. Guildbook in hand, torn between self-satisfaction at being there and dismay over his lack of ecstasy, he had quickly tired of trying to appreciate the "Old Masters." Like Newman, he turned to sprightly pictures rather than

21

somber Madonnas, and, furthermore, enjoyed the glistening copies more than the often darkened, cracked originals.

The similarity justifies James's insistence, beginning with the name of the novel as well as the hero, that Christopher Newman was highly typical. As for Twain, he won so immense a following partly because he reflected many key American attitudes: he was the favorite of the subscription-book public because he shared much of its taste, as Hamlin Hill argues. Postbellum America, especially if the rising waves of immigrants are taken into account, defied neat summary; but on the literate, middle-class level of those without any foreign accent, Twain was typical in crucial ways despite his genius. By examining his tastes in painting we can gain insights into the attitudes of the culturally dominant class. Conversely, the tastes of this class hold clues for understanding his development as a writer and, more particularly, his glaring errors in misjudging his books and his literary future. Actually, his musical tastes would tell as much, but they are not evident in such detail or stated with such color and verve as his comments on painting.

To dispose of the obvious, many of these comments slashed harshly at the old masters. In turn they have been condemned as the "most corrosive sarcasms ever hurled upon a noble subject."[1] Twain's sarcasms did strain the bounds of decorum, and also of effectiveness, as when he rhapsodized that the patterns made by camel-dung drying on the sides of houses in Syria were "frescoes" superior to those of Titian or Tintoretto. But his daring borrowed from signs that others furtively agreed with his irreverence. In *Venetian Life* (1866), William Dean Howells wished for "sincerity and boldness in saying what I thought—if I really thought anything at all—concerning the art which I spent so great a share of my time at Venice in looking at" (chapter 11). Of course some who guffawed with Twain were merely assuring themselves that what they did not understand was stupid. Some, like Howells, were releasing irritation over their inability to rise into the temple of high appreciation. Some were irritated further by indecision: they were not sure that they should enjoy any temple of the Old World; genteel culture taught that esthetic value glowed brightest in a distant and historically enriched past, but those Americans committed to roaring progress were growing confident that live value lay in the New World rather than moldy palaces and galleries. Robert G. Ingersoll, the enemy of the Biblical fundamentalists, held that emancipated man had freshness of vision in the arts also: "He prefers the modern to the old masters. . . . He gets more real pleasure from Millet and Troyon than from all the pictures of all the saints and donkeys of the Middle Ages."[2] Similarly, Ingersoll understood Twain's complaint that too many old masters showed a "cringing" and "groveling" spirit toward politically monstrous popes and princes of the dark ages.

Twain's attack on the old masters also had very practical causes. Too many of the canvases he saw were in poor condition in seedy, poorly lighted places; especially under lax nineteenth-century standards of authenticity, too many thousands of masterpieces, inflated by local pride, called for veneration. He wondered at the time if his irritation in Italy was not due mostly to the "crazy chaos," the jumbled overplus.[3] His irritation also had sources that traveled with him. We like to think of taste as a dispassionate faculty, coldly judicious, but it can be more of an interpersonal function. As the pilgrims aboard the *Quaker City* spun off into cliques, Twain soon sensed that the staid majority looked down on him as coarse and low-bred. He reacted by scorning not only their religious but also their secular pieties, by rejecting their esthetic devotions as parroted from guidebooks larded with the "easily-acquired and inexpensive technicalities of art that make such a fine show in conversation."[4] Again, with his usual verve, he only overstated what some others felt. In *Italian Journeys* (1867), published the same year that Twain's innocents toured the galleries, Howells sighed: "I am afraid that the worst form of American greenness appears abroad in a desire to be perfectly up in critical appreciation of the arts, and to approach the great works in the spirit of the connoisseur."[5]

Still, Twain had, on this score as on so many others, ambivalences beyond those that plague all of us. Aside from his symbolic antipathy toward the old masters, *The Innocents Abroad* lavished praise on many *objets d'art*.[6] The first explicit comment in the original travel letters ran, respectfully: "I loitered through the great hall of sculpture and the one hundred and fifty galleries of paintings in the palace at Versailles, and felt that to be in such a place was useless unless one had a whole year at his disposal."[7] He obviously went to Europe schooled in the assumptions that the old masters were worth looking at and that he "could not hope to become educated . . . in Europe in a few short weeks" (Book I, chapter 23). At first, anyway, the "ecstatic encomiums" of the guides raised a "gentle thrill" of feeling the "grand names of the old kings of art fall upon your ears." In short, he had learned, in the public forum rather than from any elective three-credit course, to see the traditional masters of painting as carriers of an arcane yet elevated experience. There is much talk about a culture explosion today; but its biggest stage came in the mid-nineteenth century, and Americans of skimpy background in the fine arts almost helplessly formed an ambition to level up to them.

This ambition showed up early in Twain. In 1854, when he was all of nineteen years old, his travel letters from Washington, D. C., while more interested in the patent office, insisted on noticing and even judging the local architecture, statuary, and paintings. Six years later, during his pilot days, he was trumpeting the virtues of one of Frederick E. Church's grandiloquent landscapes as the "most wonderfully beautiful painting" that St. Louis "has ever seen." Prodded by his role as a roaming columnist he had before long looked at more paintings than most Americans of a time when no city had a permanent gallery worth the name. Just before the *Quaker City* sailed he took in the show of new painting at the National Academy of Design in New York City. His note-book proves that he enjoyed it while affirming his typicality by disliking the still-lifes, bemoaning the lack of "historical" scenes, and preferring the sweetly romantic landscapes. Ominously, he commented that, though an "uncultivated vagrant," he had refused to read the exhibition catalogue and had ignored those paintings that could not speak up for themselves.

Yet, for a while at least, he did study the critical sections of guidebooks when he went abroad, and he did much more reading later. He certainly kept looking at art pieces whenever he had a chance and, emboldened rather than repelled by his first tour through the galleries of Europe, firmly planted his feet on the taste ladder. For the next thirty years, he would condescend toward levels he had already passed while both coveting and resenting those still ahead. One of the few in 1869 who had seen the treasures of Europe, he was now jeeringly superior toward the art and architecture of the Capitol.[8] As he revised for *The Innocents Abroad* he vibrated with playfulness, but he was sincere for the moment when he wrote to a fellow-passenger, who later became the wife of the competent painter, Abbott Handerson Thayer: "I have joked about the old masters a good deal in my letters, but nearly all of that will have to come out. I cannot afford to expose my want of cultivation too much. Neither can I afford to remain so uncultivated—& shall not if I am capable of rising above it."[9] Married soon himself to a genteel lady, he surprised old cronies by settling in the intellectuals' corner of Hartford, Connecticut, which had an unusual degree of artistic activity for the time. When he built his expensive house there, it went up in the Queen Anne style, then sedately avant-garde. To help furnish it his wife bought the American edition of Charles L. Eastlake's admonitory *Hints on Household Taste* as soon as it came out in 1872.

That same year he was in England, gathering notes for a travel book that never reached a first draft. The notes show that he wallowed in the current adulation of Gustav Doré, whose work "fascinated me more than anything I have seen in London yet." Doré's oil painting, twenty by thirty feet, titled *Christ Leaving the Pretorium* struck him as the "greatest work of art that ever *I* have seen by long odds" with the "only Christ . . . that was divine except Leonardo da Vinci's." Despite this bouquet to Leonardo, Twain concluded: "If Doré had lived in the time of those infernal Old Masters . . . he would have utterly eclipsed Raphael, & he would have made it warm for the Rev. Michael G. Angelo himself."[10] In London again two years later, he "spent a good part of this day browsing through the Royal Academy Exhibition of Landseer's paintings. . . . Ah, they're wonderfully beautiful!" Though art historians now speak well only of Doré's engravings and condescend to Sir Edwin Henry Landseer's sentimental, precisionist story-telling about animals, Twain's taste was elevated enough for the time, and his enthusiasm was fervent well beyond the duty of refining one's esthetic sense.

Still, the terms of that duty were complex, vague, and shifting for an uprooted, self-made intellectual. During the Gilded Age a standard antidote against such uncertainty was to talk in cash values. Twain blustered because Doré got only a "beggarly $31,500" for a painting, and he insisted that the "name of so great a man as General Grant ought not to be connected with a low-priced statue" costing less than $25,000." But, with Eastlake's help, the equating of esthetic and market value was being questioned in theory while some of the cognoscenti dared to deny it in practice. A neighbor twitted Twain "about not caring for a pretty lamp shade after he found it so very cheap—& he was vexed . . . & explained that he had no knowledge or taste himself & so when an established house said a thing was good & charged a good price for it he felt sure that it was worthy" of his wife.[12] When he tried to learn how to judge lampshades or pictures while ignoring price, confusion was the main result. Howells, not yet his friend, had summed up their mutual plight in *Venetian Life*:

> It is the sad fortune of him who desires to arrive at full perception of the true and beautiful in art, to find that critics have no agreement except upon a few loose historical principles; and that among the artists, to whom he turns in his despair, no two think alike concerning the same master, while his own little learning has made him distrust his natural likings and mislikings [chapter 11].

Besides failing to approach a consensus, art criticism had a smug, dogmatic tone that literary criticism has matched only in our generation. Twain learned to expect, primarily with dismay, that "every time I go into convulsions of admiration over a picture & want to buy it . . . some wretch who really understands art comes along & damns it."[13]

Sometimes, in less humble moods, he struck back. For example, after pretending ecstasy over an ordinary stone pediment for an iron railing, he carried on:

> . . . if you simply mention art, I cannot be calm. I can go down on my knees before one of those decayed & venerable old Masters that you have to put a sign on to tell which side of it you are looking at . . . I can *live,* in the tone and the feeling of it. Expression—expression is the thing—in art. I do not care what it expresses, & I cannot most always sometimes tell, generally, but expression is what I worship. . . .[14]

Nevertheless, he privately yearned to "like the higher music because the higher and better like it." As naively as Isabel Archer in James's *Portrait of a Lady,* he assumed that fine taste is the sign by which to recognize the aristocrats of spirit and be recognized by them as their equal. The dream of upgrading himself was not hopeless. His writing proves that he was highly sensitive to visual effects, as does his dress and personal life. In fact, he did a great deal of drawing of far beyond average competence, from youth to oldest age.[15] Half-furtively he took lessons more than once and finished some oil paintings.[16] The opening page of *A Tramp Abroad* identifies one of its three strands as his purpose "to study art," even "to learn to paint." Though ready always to veer into clowning, he stepped up his reading of art histories as well as guidebooks during the late 1870's: the growing effectiveness of his parodies is the best proof of that. While living in Paris he consorted with an enclave of American painters and sculptors; and in all the major cities of Europe, he and his wife—like most moneyed Americans with a house to round off—browsed in shops retailing art objects.

His conversion went slowly, with much backsliding, as when he jeered: "There are artists in Arkansas today who would not have had to paint signs for a living if they had had the luck to live in the time of the old masters." His jeers rang more loudly than his praises, especially when, like Nathaniel Hawthorne, he—tardily—became outraged by the nubile Venuses and similar subjects he saw in Italy. Incidentally, in good Victorian fashion, he would suspect painters of leading deliriously wicked lives; his most obscene piece of humor, "Some Thoughts on the Science of Onanism," was for a Paris audience rich with studio artists, who were warned that a prime sign of "excessive indulgence" in onanism is a "yearning to paint pictures." Nevertheless, on his trip of the late 1870's he praised some old masters—on nonreligious subjects, mainly—and bought a Del Sarto—a copy, presumably, even if he now felt that the originals "were truly divine" when "contrasted with the copies."[17] His struggles are typified through the landscapes of J. M. W. Turner, whose sense of gravity he questioned and whose colors first made him "ill"; a few months later he again "happened" into the National Gallery in London and "became so fascinated with the Turner pictures" that he "could hardly get away."

Increasingly at first-hand ease with Europe's treasures, he reasoned in his notebook: "Don't know the rules of art—but no matter—at a public table I may criticise the dinner without being a cook."[18] His judgment grew firmer, his rapport with art greater despite his sneers at the ever-receding peak of full appreciation. Beginning in the 1880's he would mix in art circles more than literary circles for the rest of his life; though he never met Eakins or Ryder, he knew virtually every American painter of solid reputation at the time. More and more he helped the general cause along, seconding his wife, for example, in her work for the Hartford Decorative Arts Society or paying $10 in 1889 to become an "Annual Member" of the Metropolitan Museum of Art in New York City. As his largest single patronage, he subsidized Karl Gerhardt, an untutored sculptor. On February 27, 1881, he appropriately gave Gerhardt a budget ledger, soon sent him and his wife on to Paris, and supported them well for at least three years.[19] In mulling over the progress reports, Twain deferred to the judgment of his protégé's "educated critics," but in 1884 he wrote to Howells: "If you run across anybody who wants a bust, be sure & recommend Gerhardt on my say-so."

Eventually, Twain's stance toward his "little sculptor" grew assertive, fed by his sense of supplying the economic base on which the statues stood. His sense of esteem was fed also by the swelling numbers who came to do his portrait, not always at his expense. As he posed he fished for free tutoring on technical questions, especially from Frank D. Millet and Charles Noel Flagg, but he felt increasingly like a patron. From Florence, Italy, he shipped in 1879 a "Holy Family, Rembrandt and 3 Fates"—more copies, surely —but also an original by expatriate Elihu Vedder, who charged $250 for it.[20] It hung in the library of his home, swelling the proof of the Clemenses' cultured affluence. He could hardly miss acquiring that "large toleration of tone" with which Howells' Silas Lapham declared, as his architect led him in deeper and deeper: "It's just like ordering a picture of a painter. You pay him enough, and he can afford to paint you a first-class picture; and if you don't, he can't" (chapter 4). Twain's sense of becoming a patron of the arts was reinforced by his growing role in choosing the illustrations that loomed so large in the subscription books. When he turned publisher he fearlessly took on all such decisions.

His affluence led him to condescend even more as he looked back down the taste ladder. In his English notebook for 1872 he declared: "I am afraid I shall never entirely enjoy a Doré engraving again. A Doré engraving is to the painted original as a fire-fly is to the sun."[21] But the gap between an original and a mass-reproduction had just narrowed sharply with the arrival of the chromolithographic process. His neighbor, Harriet Beecher Stowe, was cajoling the middle-class housewife to bring good art into the family circle through the "chromo." Above the need for bargains, Twain could instead pontificate to "Mother" Fairbanks, who had helped tutor him during the *Quaker City* excursion: "One can cover the walls with chromos that will make a visitor want to go home—or with originals which will make him stay till *you* wish he would go home." This catchy motto worked only for the wealthy. Twain could afford the best—if he could pick it out for sure—and could be more amused than touched by the earnest interior decorating of the average "house beautiful" described in *Life on the Mississippi* or its prototype in the Grangerford parlor that Huck Finn admired so. Few readers will judge these passages the same way; in a democracy the pecking order of taste is always fierce. But on the chromo Twain was close to joining those who want to "preserve the arts inviolate from contact with the vulgar masses," who today "refuse to countenance even the best contemporary color reproductions."[22] Revealingly, Howells' condescension turned toward the other end of the economic scale, as when he commented: "Lapham had not yet reached the picture-buying stage of the rich man's development, but they decorated their house with the costliest and most abominable frescoes" (chapter 2).

In fact, good chromos sold a little high, costing usually from six to twelve dollars. More important, they could give sound quality of color and subject, especially those from the Boston firm of Louis Prang.[23] In 1885 Twain came very close to writing material for a Prang calendar and also dickered to publish a volume of his chromolithographs. Still, *A Connecticut Yankee in King Arthur's Court* (1889) obviously intended ridicule when it let Hank Morgan boast a passion for chromos (chapters 7 and 22). Then, habitually taking a much more equalitarian face abroad than at home, Twain startled a British critic with his famous "Belly and Members" letter, in which, while claiming that his talents had always aimed at the "mighty mass of the uncultivated," he passionately defended the chromo as one of the "first rounds" leading "toward appreciation of art" and even attacked the "superstition that a painting by Raphael is more valuable to the civilizations of the earth than is a chromo."[24] However, in *The American Claimant* (1892), the most tired of his novels, he settled back into a dully comic routine of making Colonel Sellers prize his chromos so much that he has copies made of *them*. The novel also had a tedious sequence about two self-schooled portraitists whose daubs thrill the plebians (chapters 2, 16, 18, 21).

At least this sequence showed a further rise in Twain's command of the clichés of the art historian and critic. Only the most intolerant—and intolerable—priests of taste can deny that he had passed beyond the catechism. With the feeling of some competence came full willingness to uphold the arts as part of man's heritage. Seeing a gallery in New Zealand that was subsidized locally, he noted: "A very creditable spirit. *We* have libraries, but not art galleries for the developing of local gift."[25] No matter how badly the French irritated him, he would respectfully hold, as in "A Little Note to Paul Bourget," that they "teach us all the fine arts" with the "ablest masters in the world." By 1893 it seemed natural to set "Is He Living or Is He Dead?" in France. This fantasy sums up how far he had progressed since his "Legend of the Capitoline Venus" of 1869.

The "Legend of the Capitoline Venus," set in Rome, briskly runs through a hoax worked on behalf of an American sculptor. One of his statues is battered and then buried; when it turns up "sadly stained by soil and the mold of ages," it sells as a masterpiece. Rather than belittling the classical sculptors—whom Twain had praised invariably even when lambasting the old masters—this "Legend" complained that the genius usually goes unheralded in his lifetime. However, Twain's sculptor retires after this coup to become merely a bumbling husband and father. "Is He Living or Is He Dead?" was pegged on the real-life prestige of Jean François Millet (1814-75), then held a titan for *The Angelus* as well as other canvases.[26] A coterie of fellow painters agree to work up a boom for Millet and then to drive prices much higher by staging a fake funeral; all the insiders live grandly on the profits, though Millet must stay officially deceased. "Is He Living or Is He Dead?" warns solemnly that "many a great artist has never been acknowledged until after he was starved"; sentimentally, it opens with a Hans Christian Anderson parable about a caged songbird that children forgot to feed and then buried with remorseful care. The last paragraph sums up for Millet: "This songbird was not allowed to pipe out its heart unheard and then be paid with the cold pomp of a big funeral."

The change in basic tone between these two pieces—written almost twenty-five years apart—tells something crucial about Twain. He pondered dismayingly little about art in any form as making a unique kind of discourse and, most of his life, shied away from conceiving of his writing in such terms. To the extent that he had a guiding pattern of esthetic values, it belonged to a soft, prettified form of romanticism. His vocabulary of critical approval used "dainty," "delicate," "precious," and "heart-tugging" rather than "rebellious" or "shaggy" or "rough-hewn," much less "detached" or "ambivalent." His books, as Henry Nash Smith points out, vacillated between a vernacular and a staid, pretentious rhetoric. But without visible misgivings he assumed that *The Prince and the Pauper* soared much closer to the realm of art than *Adventures of Huckleberry Finn*. Put in terms of painting, *Huck Finn* to him was at best a cousin to genre anecdotes, which he liked but knew that the starchiest critics did not. Put in terms of music, *Huck Finn* matched his deep liking for Negro spirituals, which he enjoyed casually while fretting about rising to the challenge of Wagnerian opera. His admirers who wished that he had chosen the most elevated goals early in his career are in effect wishing away just about all of his work that is still read on its own merits. In the 1890's he did for the first time think of himself aggressively as a literary "artist." The tangible result was *Personal Recollections of Joan of Arc* (1896), surely the stiffest and emptiest of all his books.

Twain soon came to suspect this—his saving grace was the honesty to puncture his own pretensions. For that matter, he needed fewer and fewer in his closing years. Honors showered upon him; frequently he heard, at last, that he was *sui generis,* a belletrist with uniquely homespun qualities. He could indulge in that ultimate pleasure of the American who has arrived, the pleasure of being himself. This included not pretending to abilities he did not have in as full measure as he would have liked. Parading through Missouri in 1902 to accept various accolades, he spoke at a luncheon of the Art Students Association in St. Louis and confessed that he had, in greener days, "over-estimated" his capacity to "find in the old masters the joys which other people found there."

As in so many other ways, his crony Howells had followed a similar curve. In the 1880's and 1890's he toyed with sounding like a connoisseur, but in *Roman Holidays and Others* (1908) he again confessed to feeling "unequal to the ecstasies which the frescoes of Raphael and his school . . . demanded" though he did not "pride" himself on this "inability." Defensively he went on to say that "after you have been with famous works of art" you will naturally "try to believe that you have thought about them, and you should not too strictly inquire as to the fact. It is some such forbearance that accounts for a good deal of the appreciation and even the criticism of works of art" (pp. 153-54). But Twain's after-luncheon speech had a double point, which was less skeptical: ". . . if you have no natural gift for art, then it is not worth while to meddle with art. If you have a natural gift, it is not going to be valuable until you have the right teaching."[27] To prove that even the talented eye needs teaching, he recounted how his old friend and portraitist, Charles Noel Flagg, had slowly learned to see the genius of the *Mona Lisa,* which continued still to elude Twain.[28] In other words, he fittingly ended up where most American taste-climbers do: he despaired of reaching the highest level and left *that* for the experts. Still he never backed into the businessman's cliché of leaving the whole matter to his wife. Instead he was contesting her admiration for Botticelli shortly before she died;[29] though reverent toward the old masters, she had never managed to repress him seriously on that score either. The overriding point, however, is that they had habitually visited galleries in mutual seriousness.

After his wife's death, as he wandered more than ever, he settled for a while at Dublin, New Hampshire, commenting: "Any place that is good for an artist in paint is good for an artist in morals and ink."[30] He was, of course, an artist, a most uncommon one. Yet, so far as painting goes, he was, more than Christopher Newman, typical of thousands and now perhaps millions of his countrymen who see the ladder of taste shining above and try to reach the top, if only so thay can feel looked down on no longer. Ironically, scholars who spend much time on Twain get a sense of how he felt; their colleagues sometimes hint that the time would be spent better on more sophisticated writers, like Henry James. But Twain yields patterns that apply to all but the few bred in some innermost circle. With federal blessing and support, the fine arts will soon expand the call to more and more Americans to upgrade themselves culturally. Twain's experience warns them that the climb will be slow, unsure, often frustrating. They will need his sense of humor.

Notes

1. Thomas Craven, "A Cure for Critics," *Bookman,* LXVIII (Oct. 1928), 163-64.

2. "Crumbling Creeds," pp. 464-65 in *Ingersoll's Greatest Lectures* (New York, 1944).

3. *The Innocents Abroad,* Book II, chap. 1. Here and for *A Tramp Abroad* I cite the commonly available edition in the collected works.

4. *Ibid.,* Book I, chap. 19.

5. Chap. 13, "Roman Pearls."

6. Arthur L. Scott, *"The Innocents Abroad* Revaluated," *Western Humanities Review,* VII (Summer 1953), 217-20, points out some relevant passages.

7. Daniel M. McKeithan, ed., *Traveling with the Innocents Abroad* (Norman, Okla., 1958), 38.

8. "Curious Legislation and Vinnie Ream," *Mark Twain Quarterly,* V (Summer 1942), 10-11; Merle Johnson, *A Bibliography of Mark Twain* (Rev. ed., New York, 1935), 182-83.

9. Quoted in Bradford A. Booth, "Mark Twain's Friendship with Emeline Beach," *American Literature,* XIX (Nov. 1947), 228.

10. Mark Twain Papers (University of California, Berkeley—hereafter cited as MTP), DV 69. Copyright, Mark Twain Company, 1966.

11. Twain to Karl Gerhardt, July 6, 1885; letter in Yale University Library.

12. Quoted in Kenneth Andrews, *Nook Farm: Mark Twain's Hartford Circle* (Cambridge, Mass., 1950), 86.

13. Henry Nash Smith and William M. Gibson, eds., *Mark Twain-Howells Letters* (Cambridge, Mass., 1960), I, 65.

14. Bernard DeVoto, ed., *Letters from the Earth* (New York, 1962), 177. I follow the text of the original manuscript (MTP).

15. For samples or comment see Minnie M. Brashear, *Mark Twain: Son of Missouri* (Chapel Hill, 1934), 112, 116; Ferris Greenlet, *The Life of Thomas Bailey Aldrich* (Boston, 1908), plate between pp. 114-15; Twain's letter of December 25, 1880, to Mrs. Charles Dudley Warner—in Berg Collection of New York Public Library; Johnson, *A Bibliography of Mark Twain,* 158-59; Elizabeth Wallace, *Mark Twain and the Happy Island* (Chicago, 1913), 89; Philipp Mechling, "Mark Twain in Heidelberg" *Twainian,* IX (Nov.-Dec. 1950), 3; MTP, Paine 27.

16. Samuel Webster, ed., *Mark Twain, Business Man* (Boston, 1946), 21; Dan De Quille, "Reporting with Mark Twain," *Californian,* IV (July

1893), 171; Max Lederer, "Mark Twain in Vienna," *Mark Twain Quarterly,* VII (Summer-Fall 1945), 10. However, Twain's listing in *A Tramp Abroad* of the German painters under whom he had recently studied is a hoax.

17. *A Tramp Abroad* (Book II, Chapter 19).

18. MTP, Notebook #14 (Feb. 26—Sept. 8, 1879). Copyright, Mark Twain Company, 1966.

19. Twain's letters to Gerhardt are in the Yale University Library.

20. Regina Soria, "Mark Twain and Vedder's Medusa," *American Quarterly,* XVI (Winter 1964), 602-6

21. MTP, DV 69. Copyright, Mark Twain Company, 1966.

22. John A. Kouwenhoven, *Made in America* (New York, 1948), 138-39.

23. Elizabeth R. and Joseph Pennell, *Lithography and Lithographers* (New York, 1915), 217; Frank L. Mott, *A History of American Magazines, 1865-1885* (Cambridge, Mass., 1938), 182, and *A History of American Magazines, 1885-1905* (Cambridge, Mass., 1957), 17-18.

24. Albert Bigelow Paine, ed., *Mark Twain's Letters* (New York, 1917), II, 525-28.

25. MTP, Notebook #27 (March 6—Dec. 13, 1895). Copyright, Mark Twain Company, 1966.

26. Privately, Twain enjoyed the play upon the name of his old friend and portraitist, Frank D. Millet.

27. Quoted in Cyril Clemens, *Mark Twain the Letter Writer* (Boston, 1932), 112-16.

28. The anecdote about Flagg was used in 1891 for "Down the Rhone." But Arthur L. Scott, *"The Innocents Adrift* edited by Mark Twain's Official Biographer," *PMLA,* LXXVIII (June 1963), 234-35, points out that Twain had then put it into the mouth of a character with whom he was mostly disagreeing.

29. Raffaele Simboli, "Mark Twain from an Italian Point of View," *Critic,* XLIV (June 1904), 523.

30. Hartford (Conn.) *Courant,* Nov. 25, 1905.

A Tale of Two Authors:
Theodore Dreiser and David Graham Phillips

Louis Filler

During Dreiser's first critical emergence, it was natural to compare his version of American life with that which he was apparently opposing, though this was often done by indirection. Dreiser was held to be telling the truth, in contrast to authors of what was called the "sweetness and light" school. Dreiser was not *directly* contrasted with the muckrakers, and it needs to be emphasized that Dreiser was not (as some textbook writers have imagined) a muckraker. Nor could he be associated with his fellow-Hoosier, David Graham Phillips. Their methods and goals seemed so patently different as scarcely to warrant explication. H. L. Mencken was in the 1910's a leading figure in the controversies which revolved about novelists and their achievements. It is needless to abstract or footnote his well-known defenses of Dreiser and Dreiser's works. More relevant would be his view of Phillips, as recorded in his *Prejudices* (1919), which saw him as one who "with occasional revisions to honest work, devoted most of his later days to sensational serials for the train-boy magazines. . . . [W]hen he died his desk turned out to be full of them, and they kept dribbling along for three or four years. . . ."

Since this passage, written even after the publication and storm of Phillips's *Susan Lenox: Her Fall and Rise,* deals with the American Winston Churchill and with Robert W. Chambers, as well as with Phillips, it should be evident what kind of complex of writers Mencken was conjuring up, and how it might seem to contrast with one involving Dreiser. In the light of this 1919 estimate of Phillips by Mencken, it is of interest to consider a more extended opinion set down by Mencken in 1910, when Phillips seemed to him "The Leading American Novelist":

You will find in [Phillips] two qualities so rare in contemporary American fiction that the reader of current novels seldom encounters even faint traces of them. One is the quality of earnestness and the other is the quality of intelligence. Mr. Phillips writes as if novel-writing were a serious business, demanding preparation, reflection, ardor, skill. He seems to be firmly convinced that the people whose doings he is describing are real human beings, that their overt acts are the effects of deep-lying motives and causes, and that it is worthwhile to tunnel down into them and get all these motives and causes. He thinks! Contemplating his characters, he is led to meditate and philosophize upon the internal and external *stimuli* which make them what they are. And passing from what they are to what they represent, he investigates the general conditions of human existence in the United States, differentiating between things universal and things American, ferreting out material weaknessess, prying into the peculiar customs, vices, superstitions, emotions, traditions and diatheses which separate an American from an Englishman, a Zulu, or the bisque hero of a best-seller.

The man, of course, is an anarchist. Such earnestness is revolutionary, dangerous, insulting, abominable. The purpose of novel-writing as that crime is practiced in the United States is not to interpret life—to make it a merry round of automobiling, country clubbing, seduction, money-making, and honey-mooning with music by Victor Herbert. Novelists succeed among us in proportion as they keep outside the skin. But Mr. Phillips does not bid for success that way. He boldly ventures upon haphazard psychological laparotomies, he insists upon making indecent cross-sections of the American woman; he looks for the roots of ideals, not in the heart, but in the stomach; he orates vociferously all the while he is at work. The first impression he produces is that he is merely a noisy and lawless fellow; the second is that his remarks are interesting but untrue; the last is that, whether true or false, they are at least worth heeding and hearing, as the conclusions of a man who has approached his task seriously, who has brought with it an excellent technical equipment, and whose efforts to accomplish something worth while are sincere, dignified and praiseworthy.

There is no gain in further recapitulating examinations of Phillips as a novelist or person by Ludwig Lewisohn, Oscar Cargill, and others of critical status or influence. I have examined this subject in an article, "The Reputation of David Graham Phillips."[1] More interesting would be the attitudes toward Dreiser as artist and observer by those who, in and out of academic circles, found him worthy of derogation during the first wave of debate. A remarkable reminiscence by Dreiser himself merits notice because his subject, Stuart P. Sherman, was both in and out of academic life and has received regard in both capacities:

I first heard of Sherman from an editorial writer on the *Indianapolis Star,* I forget his name. But previous to his being an editor on the *Star,* as he told me, he had been assistant professor of English under Sherman at Urbana. And not only that, but Sherman had caused him to be discharged. And on account of me and my books! For somewhere back in 1913 or 1914, he said, he had come across several of my books and had become an enthusiastic exponent of the same, discussing their significance in his classes, and urging students to read them, and later, according to him, there were pro-Dreiser freshmen and sophomores, a college newspaper mention of the same, and finally the troubled attention of Professor Sherman. For he was my young editor's superior.

"One day," said this man, "Sherman walked into my lecture room and asked me who this man Dreiser was. What books he had written. Why was I so enthusiastic? And then learning that I had copies of *Sister Carrie, Jennie Gerhardt, The Financier,* etc., he asked for the loan of them—took them away with him. Some weeks later there was trouble for me, for he came back to say that he did not think the books were decent, and more, they did not merit the emphasis I was placing on them. They were vulgar, brutal, immoral, and as such, subversive of all the best tendencies in our literature, and that he was personally going to attack Dreiser on that ground."

Not only that, but he also indicated to his assistant [*sic*] that he would prefer it if no further mention of Dreiser were made, unless it were condemnatory. But since this young editor was not a little courageous and even defiant and continued to discuss my books, he was dropped.[2]

It may be charitably argued that Sherman's cowardly and bullying attitude was later compensated for by his famous turnabout which placed him on the side of Dreiser, Sherwood Anderson, and others who were especially interested in extending the borders of discussion of man-woman relations. The question is, however, whether the grounds for Sherman's original distaste any longer help to distinguish Dreiser from Phillips. That Dreiser has a "pioneer" status in the depiction of sex relations no one would deny, but this would constitute small pickings indeed from the harvest of Dreiser's fame, and would even have to be shared with Phillips himself. Dreiser, in a letter to the present author, conceded that *Susan Lenox,* as a topic, was "remarkable and original at the time it was written." But, in the light of his own present reputation, it is almost ludicrous that he would go on to indict Phillips as lacking "the sense of poetry, and beauty, and artistic coherence, which better writers have." By the late 1930's, Dreiser had come to believe himself unknown in America, and during World War II all his books were out of print. He became subject to that phenomenon which wants understanding in connection with other American fiction writers, as well as himself: his popularity in the Soviet Union, during a time when his popularity among his very own countrymen was in decline.

By 1950, a literary milieu which made much of Henry James and T. S. Eliot found little use for the now deceased Dreiser. His position in academia was substantially what it had been in the 1910's, with no equivalent of H. L. Mencken about to represent a forceful dissident opinion. James T. Farrell, one of Dreiser's direct heirs, became almost a barometer of naturalism in this time. His steady and then precipitous decline in prestige has finally left him almost totally without literary reputation. The meaning of these developments is yet to be clarified, but Robert Spiller is suggestive in his *The Cycle of American Literature* (1955):

> The attack of the literary radicals [begun, it should be recalled, in the 1910's] was forceful, but it could not be long sustained because it was based on no agreed idea, values, or program. That of a smaller group, known as the neohumanists, was more effective because it formulated and preached a limited set of doctrines.

Doubtless objective events and popular tendencies aided the neohumanists, but, whatever the reason, their victory was overwhelming in terms of Dreiser's substantial influence. True, he has his memorialists. But the Kazin, Shapiro-edited *The Stature of Theodore Dreiser* (1955) underscores how purely historical it is, when appreciative, and how minimal when it aspires to show striking force in the present. Lionel Trilling's estimate of Dreiser, reprinted in this volume, seems strategic, in view of this critic's own contemporary stature, and because the humanistic premises he fancies constitute so drastic a criticism of his own radical intellectual past. Trilling's sweeping derogation of Dreiser as a "failure of mind and heart" leaves little left but historical recrimination, and not even so much of the lowly Dreiser as of his so-called liberal admirers of bygone decades.

Dreiser fares better in the hands of Charles Shapiro, whose *Theodore Dreiser: Our Bitter Patriot* (1962) seeks to save his art from himself. But at what a cost! Dreiser's *The "Genius"* rests on a "faulty base . . . of capitalism and eroticism" (pp. 4, 60). His wealthy people are "abstract monsters of unreality" (p. 15). Dreiser is "over-sentimental" (p. 17). And so on and on. His *The Financier* is held, "if nothing else," to "present us with a staggering amount of documented material on the intricate machinations involved in capturing and controlling the traction lives of American and English cities" (p. 26)—praise which Dreiser's literary detractors would be glad to read and quote with complacence.

Finally, it would seem fair to say that as a factor in creative fiction of today, Dreiser has no more status or stature than David Graham Phillips himself. A collection of essays on the "living novel," published in 1957, includes such representative talents as Saul Bellow, Ralph Ellison, and Herbert Gold, among many others. These fiction-writers find reason to discuss Herman Melville and Mark Twain. They wander as far afield as Smollett and Tolstoi. They make much, repeatedly, of Ernest Hemingway and F. Scott Fitzgerald, and of Thomas Wolfe, D. H. Lawrence, James Joyce, Henry James, and William Faulkner. They find not one single passing occasion to mention Dreiser.

There may, then, be less separating Phillips from Dreiser than was evident to H. L. Mencken in 1919. It is obvious, in retrospect, that both served Mencken's purposes, rather than their own. In 1910, when Mencken wrote his *Smart Set* article, he imagined Phillips helpful to his own perspective on man and Americans. Dreiser's emergence as an *enfant terrible* enabled Mencken to dispense with Phillips as a useful literary commodity. There are, to be sure, still individuals about who find Dreiser fairly useful. Thus, one student of the city in fiction credits him with "realizing" the twentieth-century city, despite his crudeness, lack of unity, and of form. What does this realization comprehend?

> Dreiser's heroes are a radical departure from literary tradition. Emotionally intense, romantic, and sensual, they are all driven by instinct rather than reason or duty; they are highly amoral; they rarely, if ever, achieve spiritual stature; and they all live through a tragic pattern that brings them to inner defeat.[3]

There is more to this analysis of "a key figure in American city fiction," who is said to have "revealed and deplored the wasteland elements in the twentieth-century world." But it suffices that this is a mere monograph which must deal with city fiction because that is its thesis, and which presumes to judge Dreiser's alleged strengths and weaknesses by the measure of the author's own view of what constitutes a true version of reality. Thus, she is critical of Will Payne's *The Story of Eva* (which Dreiser happened to admire), because, in her words, "there is a happy ending complete with reformations in character and wedding bells." Happy endings are unreal. H. B. Fuller's *The Cliff-Dwellers,* also tenderly kept in Dreiser's recollections, was also written down because "the pattern of characterization and plot (the moral nature of the hero, the penance for crime, and the victorious emergence from sordid experience) keeps it within the conventions of the nineteenth century novel." People do not emerge victorious from sordid experience. During Dreiser's ascendency, David Graham Phillips was often accused of perpetrating happy endings, and thus adding to contrived and unrealistic fiction. This study of the American city novel, crude and imperceptive though it be, helps remind us of what the Dreiser legend once was, and once implied. It can help us no more. Happy endings or sad ones can no longer explain an author. General approval or disapproval, be it of Dreiser or of Phillips, can no longer compensate for inadequate explication of style or substance.

There are factors which can help create a comparison between these novelists, explaining their differences in personality and development. It is possible that such a comparison can redound to Dreiser's better appreciation in the present. Or it might not. The area has been too little worked to permit too firm a prediction. The following notes would have to be expanded before one could say confidently what conclusions they could lead to.

For one thing, as has already been mentioned, both novelists were from Indiana. Although Phillips came of English stock and Dreiser of immigrant German, both shared opportunities to think well of their native soil. After all, there have been happy Hoosiers of German stock, and even happy authors among them. Phillips' father was a well-established banker in Madison, Indiana, beautifully situated on the Ohio River, and young Phillips was raised in a happy home. Dreiser, despite his father's rigidly religious nature, had similar prospects before him. For his father owned a woolen mill in Sullivan, Indiana, and their home was ruled over by a tolerant and loving mother. Fire destroyed the family fortunes, and the Dreisers made a series of moves which increased their family chaos. Incidentally, Dreiser exploited almost every aspect of his personal experiences, in fiction and autobiography. Phillips, with some indirect exceptions, firmly distinguished between his personal life and his contribution as a novelist. Materials relating to him have been steadily disappearing over the past fifty years, and soon many aspects of his affairs will be totally beyond recall.

How universal were Dreiser's experiences as a child and youth? They were characterized by drift and by stumbling responses to the loose social circumstances which he encountered in the Indiana towns he inhabited, in Chicago, and at Indiana University. At one early point in his life, he inhabited with his family a cottage owned by his brother Paul's mistress, who was also a madam. Phillips was raised more decorously by literate parents concerned for culture and history, but also in circumstances which might best be termed small-town. There is no record of chaos or rebellion in Phillips' early life, and there was no occasion for either. Madison had "four flouring mills, three iron foundries with machine shops, one brass foundry, several planing mills, and a dry dock. The building of steamboats is an important branch of industry here." Phillips later expressed his democratic satisfaction with Madison's public schools, though he also benefited from private tutoring. At fifteen, in 1882, accompanied by his mother, Phillips, a fast-growing, plump boy came to Asbury College, later De Pauw University. The next year, he took courses at the University of Cincinnati, while living in the home of his married sister. He then returned to Asbury. In 1885, he entered Princeton University, or the College of New Jersey as it then was. In none of these institutions did Phillips make any signal record. At Asbury, he indicated that he might wish to become a banker. Yet he took only liberal arts courses, read Zola, and somehow made contact with George Gissing's *Demos*. He seems to have been earnest and argumentative; "La Bouche," some fellow-students called him at Princeton.

His entrance into newspaper work reveals curious similarities and dissimilarities, as compared with Dreiser's.

Dreiser depicts himself as a weak, confused boy with a tenuous job as a collector of small commercial debts, who nevertheless harbored a good opinion of himself. " 'No common man am I,' I was constantly saying to myself, and I would no longer be held down to this shabby world of collecting in which I found myself." By degrees, Dreiser had "come to feel a great contempt for the average mind." He saw himself as "a sort of nondescript dreamer without the power to earn a decent living and yet with all the tastes and proclivities of one destined to an independent fortune. My eyes were constantly fixed on people in positions far above my own. Those who interested me most were bankers, millionaires, artists, executives, leaders, the real rulers of the world." He imagined he could be a writer, though he had made no serious efforts at writing, and had once sent "a bundle of incoherent MS" to Eugene Field of the Chicago *Daily News,* which had certainly been consigned to the trash bin. Dreiser now shrewdly decided to try the least notable Chicago paper, the *Daily Globe,* "a struggling affair financed by one of the Chicago politicians for political purposes only."

Told that there was no job for him, Dreiser took to hanging on in the "large, bare room" where the editors worked and the reporters came and went. His persistence and ignorance touched the copy-reader, John Maxwell, who, in 1892, gave him a chance to cover the Democratic Convention then meeting in their city. By blundering good-fortune, Dreiser scored a remarkable "beat" for his paper, and so secured himself among the cynics and adventurers who inhabited the newspaper business.

A young man of nineteen, fresh from Princeton, over six feet three and brashly dressed in "dude" fashion, and with a cigarette perpetually drooping from his lips, Phillips had almost less to offer than Dreiser did to a hard-headed newspaper editor of this era. Phillips' entrance into journalism was, for a time, one of the minor sagas of the newspaper world. Its main qualities were perceived as involving hard work and brilliant versatility. But it shows other characteristics as well. Phillips' associates at Princeton were, of course, scions of the people Dreiser adored from afar. And their prospects rarely led them into the newspaper field, at least on the reportorial level. Phillips did ask a son of publisher Murat Halstead to introduce him to his father's editor on the Cincinnati *Commercial,* but this did him no good. The editor cared nothing for Phillips' liberal arts education.

Neither did the editor of the Cincinnati *Times-Star.* Phillips proceeded to set up a siege. Day after day he sat in the office reading exchange newspapers and enduring the glances of the regular *Times-Star* reporters and office-boys. It was a humiliating period. Dreiser later—he was four years younger than Phillips —felt like a homeless cat hanging "about a doorstep for days and days meowing to be taken in." Phillips must have felt more like a South Sea Islander being exhibited at a fair. Yet he was only some sixty miles from home, where dignity and support waited for him.

Phillips "made it" on his own. A story arrived for the editor's disposal with all the reporters out in the field. Desperately, he asked Phillips to get the facts; they would be written up in the office. Phillips returned with the facts, and also with a written account of his own, put together expertly and in the *Times-Star* manner. The editor looked the tall youngster over again and realized that he had a first-class newspaperman before him.

But though Phillips was soon known as one of Cincinnati's best reporters, he never relaxed his manner or attitude. He never enjoyed competitiveness. He never learned to use influence or prestige. Though his personal papers reveal uncertainties, sympathies, tolerances, his formal regard was for strength and performance. Even informally, he esteemed hard work and endurance as guarantors of independence and freedom: the sole assurance of sustenance in a Darwinian world.

When, three years later, Phillips decided to challenge New York, his tactics were the same, though he was now a well-established journalist with numerous newspaper associates. He acquired work, briefly, on the *Tribune,* then on the *Sun,* where he was given relatively modest assignments. He proved himself with one of those reports which startle the entire newspaper fraternity. Phillips was soon able to account himself a success, first with Dana's anti-reform *Sun,* then, more comfortably, with Joseph Pulitzer's Democratic *World.*

Yet there is a sharp strain of pessimism in much that he thought and experienced during this period. In 1891, he broke out of unqualified journalese to publish no fewer then ten pieces, one a story, in *Harper's Weekly.* They are revealing for their general tone of bleakness and discouragement. Phillips tells the attentive reader elsewhere of how a young writer could begin first chapters of novels, and first scenes of first acts of plays, and give them up for lack of direction. In general, it can be observed that his strong individualism required independence and security for comfort, but that he found ordinary success with its ordinary perspectives of material satisfaction and emulation insufficient for his psychic needs. In general, too, it can be noted that he hungered for a faith in democracy and human kindness, such as he had experienced in Madison and at home, but which he perceived to be old-fashioned and incompetent so far as the new industry and the new urban civilization were concerned. His problem was to forge a philosophy which would cope with them, as well as with the bitter facts of human nature which his daily work displayed.

Dreiser, on the other hand, hungered frankly for material satisfaction, sexual joys, and prestige. Though somewhat burdened by philosophical questions, they did not impede his quest, during his first years of professional work. As soon as finances permitted, he wore clothes which were more absurd than Phillips'. Dreiser was ready to write anything his editors expected. From Chicago, he went on to St. Louis, and then back to Chicago, plagued especially by sexual desires, and saddened by the confused living and tragedy which his personal and newspaper experiences revealed. He developed the amoral view of human relations which was later to please his defenders and outrage his critics. In terms of the observations which one might desire in a novelist concerned for American terrain and American circumstances—as distinguished from the cerebral, though presumably universal and essential details preferred by a Henry James—Dreiser did very well, ranging among the cities he explored for opportunities on his way to New York.

Phillips was a student of events. He pondered the meaning of ordinary life and ordinary mortals, and in many columns and reportorial notes sought to generalize their meaning. He found it difficult, and perhaps disheartening, to concentrate on futile and deteriorated personalities, and he took seriously, critically, the personalities of such famous Americans as William Jennings Bryan and Grover Cleveland. Dreiser also professed an interest in the activities of the great, but his writings leave little residue, so far as their programs or intrinsic significance are concerned. His admirers would later hold that Dreiser cut beneath the surface, accumulating a wide range of vignettes of ordinary people whom he met or noticed in his travels and utilizing them in his fiction and personal memoirs. Thus, he quoted almost without change in The "Genius" and also in A Book About Myself a sad note written him by the woman who became his first wife. Frank Harris thought that ordinary people interested Phillips—his gallery reminded Harris of Franz Hals's portraits—but, certainly, they lacked the detailed element of drift and futility which Dreiser imparted to his subjects.

Dreiser, in a much-quoted passage, has told how he was met in New York with discouraging rejections by various newspaper editors:

> I finally went to City Hall Park, which fronted the majority of them . . . and stared at their great buildings. About me was swirling the throng which has always made that region so interesting, the vast mass that bubbles upward from the financial district and the regions south of it and crosses the plaza to Brooklyn Bridge and the elevated roads (the subways had not come yet). About me on the benches of the park was, even in this gray, chill December weather, that large company of bums, loafers, tramps, idlers, the flotsam and jetsam of the great city's whirl and strife to be seen there today. I presume I

looked at them and then considered myself and these great offices, and it was then that the idea of *Hurstwood* was born.

Elsewhere, in an even better-known passage, Dreiser tells of his discovery of Herbert Spencer, "whose introductory volume to his *Synthetic Philosophy (First Principles)* quite blew me, intellectually, to bits." This totally forgotten work will, no doubt, ultimately want explication in order to help define its effect upon Dreiser, and Phillips, and all of their generation. For there can be no question but that Phillips was also affected by its evolutionary premises.

The crucial fact was the difference it, and other influences—for its remarkable vogue no more than meshed with other objective facts of life, as they seemed to present themselves for assimilation—made in the viewpoints of Dreiser and of Phillips. It informed the dreary end of *Hurstwood,* whose corpse, with that of many another down-and-out suicide, was conveyed by municipal scow for anonymous burial in Potter's Field. It informed the dreary ending of *Jennie Gerhardt,* who was left alone to live out a few more meaningless years and disappear. Phillips took a more agnostic view of the predicament in which evolutionary theory had left him. For those who imagine him to be a passionless or sentimental journalist in fiction, there are surprises of tremulous and troubled writing in his unpublished papers.

But more decisive was his difference with Dreiser in social outlook. Dreiser could only look to himself for satisfaction and sympathy. He could only mourn helplessly and inconsolably for man's fate. This, ultimately, satisfied many readers who could respond empathetically to the dilemma he posed, and also, remarkably, received the approval of their opposites: apparently principled and programmed socialists and communists who took his work to be a faithful expose of a corrupt and dying capitalism.

This viewpoint gave no satisfaction to Phillips. He had a broad tolerance for human frailty and defeat, asking, in one passage, whether we were not all failures sketched by nature on the blackboard and sponged impatiently away. He expressed admiration for Oscar Wilde's mind, even after his fall. But Phillips needed a sense of man's capacity to cope with life and with the enigmas of life. The turmoil and tragedy which Dreiser was content to feel and report disturbed Phillips only to the extent that it was not controlled. "Man," he later wrote, "is not a fallen angel, but a rising animal." A passage in his first novel, *The Great God*

Success, published a year after *Sister Carrie's* disastrous release, adequately records Phillips' frame of reference. It quite evidently takes off from the great Bryan effort of 1896, which Phillips took with intense seriousness. Subsequent events—the Klondike Gold Rush, the "great little" war with Spain—pleased Phillips much less than it did many of his contemporaries. He considered that the battle was joined—the battle against Privilege and for "a restoration of government by the people. The candidates were nominated, the platforms put forward and the issue squarely joined."

And now, in 1902, such a time actually went under way beyond the dreams of Phillips and Charles Edward Russell and Upton Sinclair and many others who had found the "bitch-goddess of success" a charmless companion. Phillips left newspaper work entirely and began the extraordinary production of novels, stories, articles, and other writings which made him a contemporary legend, and which is yet to be reasonably estimated. Neither *The Treason of the Senate* nor *Susan Lenox: Her Fall and Rise* can be usefully evaluated apart from the Progressive and muckraking tenets from which they stemmed.

But what was Dreiser about in this period? In the 1890's, following a brief and ignominious contact with the New York *World,* where Phillips was a star editor and reporter, Dreiser became editor of *Ev'ry Month,* a magazine which pandered freely to care-less-minded readers. He became a successful writer of magazine articles which exploited docile formulas on any and every random theme. Dreiser frankly enjoyed the fruits of his easy writing and made little effort to learn discipline or refine style. He seems to have drifted into the writing of *Sister Carrie,* but had high hopes for it. Its great failure crushed him. When he had found himself again—his breakdown and despair were once a theme for literary sympathy—it was with determination to grasp security firmly. It is an interesting comment on the character of literary fads that details of his rather untidy personal life, as well as of his unprincipled journalistic career, were not similarly studied and assayed. In 1905-6, Dreiser edited *Smith's Magazine,* one of the less distinguished periodicals of the time. His next job, as editor of the *Broadway Magazine,* saw him espousing only "that which is sweet and refreshing, and clean." From 1907 to 1910, he served as editor-in-chief of the Butterick Publications, comprising *Delineator, Designer, New Idea,* and others. Charles Hanson Towne, a versifier and editor of the time, recalls how earnestly

Dreiser warned him against deviating to any degree from their editorial formulas for holding readers' attention. Dreiser, of course, distinguished between bread-winning and art, and his viewpoint constituted an indirect criticism of muckraking art as specious and ill-founded. For various reasons, some of which have been implied, Dreiser, during his years as an established literary figure, suffered less critically than did Phillips from the fact that he had been a figure in journalism. Recently, however, as in such a condemnatory and grossly irresponsible a treatment as Kenneth S. Lynn's *The Dream of Success* (1955)—itself successful among academicians—Dreiser's earlier advantage has been lost. Dreiser is limned as worshipful and undiscriminating before material power, and worthless in its literary treatment of it. His tragic vision of life is not separated from that which enabled him to survive and function in capitalistic America.[4]

Phillips's notoriety ended abruptly, as did the muckraking movement which gave him his platform for work. His critics Granville Hicks and Lynn, with that curious inhumanity all too often found among alleged humanists, treat his tragic and courageous death with distressing lack of appreciation and common decency. But, until at least 1911, the year he was assassinated, there were literary, personal, and philosophical comparisons possible between Dreiser and Phillips. Indeed, the period can be profitably extended to include most of the 1910's. For this is the era of the youth movement, the era of Randolph Bourne, John Reed, Van Wyck Brooks, the era which saw the emergence of Sherwood Anderson, Edgar Lee Masters, and others who have figured in our recollections, or, as in the case of Masters, are figuring again. They affected the reception of Dreiser's works of that era, notably *The "Genius,"* and of Phillips' posthumous novels and stories, culminating in 1917 in the publication of *Susan Lenox*. Indeed, interesting comparisons could be made of the critical receptions of both *The "Genius"* and *Susan Lenox*. Whatever one might think of these novels as art, there is no doubt that such studies would throw much light on the standards and intentions of their critics.

Many other points of comparison between Phillips and Dreiser suggest themselves. I mention their personal lives only because they have been handled so cavalierly by persons interested in making a quick allegation or judgment, and not over-reverent in handling data or inferences. Dreiser, for all his licentious thinking and activity, had a conventional side to his nature. He dreamed of a peaceful and settled life, before coming to New York, and investigated the possibility of linking marriage with the life of a small-town Ohio newspaper proprietor. He did marry, and lived many years in that state before his restless spirit caused him to beg his wife to divorce him. Through much of his later life, he had a constant companion whom he married shortly before his death. Phillips, in the meantime, as a young man kept a mistress in circumstances which he viewed as a "Bohemian quicksand," though they were sedate enough. This liaison was the love of his life, and he seems to have suffered pangs of conscience, perhaps induced by her death. Phillips never married, and appears never to have taken any later relations seriously. He was best known for his life-long association with one of his sisters, a divorcée who kept his Gramercy Park apartment for him until his death.

All such matters can doubtless throw light on Dreiser's and Phillips' particular purposes or writings or convictions. They wait, however, for significance on the more vital problem of literary validity. How to define terms which can make for critical validity? No person of wisdom will deny the importance of spontaneous popularity or unpopularity. But he will wish also to understand the difference between writing which has historical import, and writing which moves and persuades someone today. And he will wish to sharpen his own understanding so that he can present it scrupulously and in a fashion enabling him to learn from others. Phillips and Dreiser were both actors in a drama of intellectual effort which can inform our present cultural circumstances. Seen apart, as individual authors, they have as much to tell us, surely, as do Edward Eggleston, Booth Tarkington, and others who have received scholarly attention. Seen together, Dreiser and Phillips have something of a cultural nature to tell us.

Notes

1. *Antioch Review,* Winter 1951-52, 475-88.
2. Helen Dreiser, *My Life with Dreiser* (Cleveland, 1951), 78.
3. Blanche H. Gelfant, *The American City Novel* (Norman, Okla., 1954), 63, 66, 94.
4. For an analysis, see my "Dreamers and the American Dream," *Southwest Review* (Autumn 1955), 359 ff.

John Hersey:
War Correspondent Into Novelist

David Sanders

On May 8, 1945—V-E Day—John Hersey won the Pulitzer Prize for his first novel, *A Bell for Adano*. Twenty years later, with the appearance of his eleventh book, *White Lotus*, he has been told that while he once aspired to have a silver tongue, he has been given instead a golden touch; that instead of writing literature for all time, he has written books that make the Book-of-the-Month Club. Hersey should not have been discouraged by such remarks. They might have been said of any recent American novelist who had published several widely read novels on subjects of immediate social or historical interest. These remarks are passingly ironic only because they were made by someone employed, as Hersey once was, by *Time*.

In order to have been judged more favorably, Hersey could have blocked out a careful ground of personal experience from his missionary childhood in China to some point in his adult life and then written a WASP novel, without guilt, with just enough humor, with that special access to the theme of racial identity given only to insiders. Or he might have drawn the inescapable conclusion from everything that he reported during World War II. By adding Hiroshima to Guadalcanal, the Sicilian campaign, and the ruins of Warsaw, he should have come up with the sum of absurdity, then canceled it because of its possible consequence of revolt, and settled for meaninglessness.

Instead, he proceeded less imaginatively to become a novelist. Except in such digressions as *The Marmot Drive* and *A Single Pebble*, he has taken some of the main historical events and social problems of his time as his subjects. Habits that he ac-

49

quired as a reporter have gone into the writing of each novel, especially such habits as observation, memory, and research.

His second novel, *The Wall*, is probably the most thorough example of his method. He saw the ruins of Warsaw in 1944, then the ruins of Hiroshima in 1946. For two years he read documents of the Warsaw ghetto, had others translated for him, and listened for several hundred hours to the wire transcriptions recorded by his translators. He began a longhand draft as he listened to these recordings and then abandoned it because of the strange effect these recordings were having upon him. He finished a second draft after making a crucial change in response to that effect. This is the barest possible outline of how this journalist wrote what is probably his best novel; this sketch will be filled in after we have seen what kind of a journalist he was when he began writing it. Let us also be certain that *The Wall* is a novel, although "epic," "monument," and "indictment" were terms that came more readily to the people who praised it. Others called it "fictionalized journalism."

The Wall is the story of the Jews of the Warsaw ghetto during World War II. It begins with the German occupation in the fall of 1939 and ends as the last survivors of the resistance movement escape extermination in 1943. It is told in the form of a scholar's journal, the "Levinson archive," as detailed a record as Hersey might be expected to produce after all his preparation. Fact and history go directly into this fiction, but not at the expense of fiction. The novel is dominated by the brilliantly imagined character of Noach Levinson—though characterization is not consistently Hersey's strength as a novelist. Levinson, the archivist, becomes someone—a complex and compelling person—in the course of making his entries, and he comes to see far more in the characters of his acquaintances than their responses to ghetto conditions. Nor does Hersey's stubbornly acquired knowledge of what happened in the ghetto between 1939 and 1943 crowd out his understanding of how these events are related to the centuries of Jewish history since the Diaspora or keep him from convincing his readers of the timelessness of the theme of survival. *The Wall* is a novel about the events of the Warsaw ghetto as told by a wholly fictional narrator. And *The War Lover* is a novel about the conflicting impulses toward life and death that may be found in wartime aviators, *The Child Buyer* is a novel about the abuse of high intelligence in the American public-school system, and *White Lotus* is a novel about the psychology of an oppressed race.

Hersey has written these novels and three others, and yet seems less a novelist to many critics and reviewers than does the author of *Catch-22* or novelists such as Norman Mailer and James Jones. I have mentioned Hersey's choice of subjects as one reason for his situation, and certainly another might be his affirmative response to some of these subjects. Still another will be found in the praise he has been given. No one has ever condemned *Hiroshima*, a book still always referred to as "inspired journalism." In fact, no one seems to have found adequate words for praising it. It gave millions of American readers their first knowledge of the human suffering caused by the first atomic bomb; before it, they had known nothing about the explosion but statistics and photographs of mushroom clouds. Albert Einstein is said to have ordered a thousand copies of the famous issue of the *New Yorker* to distribute among his fellow townsmen in Princeton. Bernard Baruch ordered another thousand. Very few books have ever been urged upon people so suddenly and so imperatively, certainly not the wartime books, including Hersey's own *Into the Valley*, which the Office of War Information had called "imperative reading." *Hiroshima* has been praised more often as a deed than as a book. In whatever Hersey would go on to write, he would be marked by the "earnestness of his intentions"—not a novelist's earnest intentions, but a prophet's. It has been assumed, furthermore, that the earnestness that went into *Hiroshima* could never go into anything else Hersey might write. So, from *The Wall* to *White Lotus*, he has written novels that have failed when they have not instead succeeded as "inspired journalism."

Many novelists have begun as reporters and then gone back into reporting in the midst of their novel-writing. Hemingway, Crane, and Dos Passos have done so without damage, but Hersey's case is not quite like theirs. His background as a war correspondent did not disqualify him as a novelist, but the peculiar circumstances of his reporting differ significantly from those of these other reporter-novelists and they are peculiarly responsible for Hersey's flying in the face of literary taste and writing novels about contemporary history. These circumstances include his employers, his media, his beats, and the Second World War.

Hersey went to work for *Time* in October 1937, after spending the summer as Sinclair Lewis' secretary. He had waited patiently for an opening on *Time* because this magazine was, he felt, "the

liveliest enterprise of its type." After a year and a half in the
New York headquarters, where he became thoroughly grounded
in *Time*style and *Time* editing (that process by which the news
became arranged as "World Affairs" or "Miscellany"), he was sent
to the Chungking bureau, a logical assignment for a man who,
like Henry Luce, was a native of Tientsin. There he began reporting the Sino-Japanese war *Time*style with dispatches on
Chungking air raids and interviews with the Generalissimo. Then
he abruptly went off to Tokyo to interview Foreign Minister
Matsuoka and United States Ambassador Joseph Grew. Reporting an air raid called for graphic details, quickly chosen and then
processed by *Time*'s formular understatement. Interviews invariably led to the significant quote. All assignments required the reporter's instant adaptation to the day's new scene, no matter
how much it might differ from the scene of the day before.
Hersey, fresh from listening to Chiang Kai-shek's plans to win the
war, could shift easily to write about Ambassador Grew's policy of
"dynamic appeasement."

Hersey was not in the Philippines during the early months of
the war, but after four and a half years of working for *Time*
he was able to put together a book called *Men on Bataan,* which
was published in June 1942. *Time*'s files, letters from servicemen,
and interviews with colleagues who had been on Bataan gave
him the material for a book, which was half about General Mac-
Arthur and half about fifty of the other 50,000 men who fought
there. Fletcher Pratt, in reviewing the book for an issue of *The
Saturday Review of Literature*—an issue devoted to the question
of wartime morale and guest-edited by Mrs. Roosevelt—said that
it "should be read by every participant in the struggle" and that
"it was literature that will not be read with shame after the war."
In 1942, this meant that *Men on Bataan* was not like *Three
Soldiers* or *A Farewell to Arms*. "You ought to know [these men]
for they are like you," Hersey wrote in the second chapter. "They
have reacted as you will react when your crisis comes, splendidly
and worthily, with no more mistakes than necessary." Although
the writer was plainly caught up in the war effort, turning out a
book for morale's sake and, as nearly as possible, for truth's sake
in a year of American defeat, he was also at the farthest point
in his recent career from his best journalism or from the possibility
of becoming a novelist.

Fortunately for his development in all respects, he was assigned
to Guadalcanal in 1942 and was privileged to observe men he would

write about. He accompanied a Marine detachment into the third battle of the Matanikau River and filled most of his next book, *Into the Valley*, with what he had seen. He was with a company when it was pinned down by sniper fire. He was in line as a false rumor of retreat was passed back eagerly from man to man. He helped to carry a litter bearing a man with a mortal abdominal wound. These things he reported, along with his own admission that if he had known what was to happen during those three days he would never have gone along. *Into the Valley* was honest reporting that anticipated *Hiroshima*, even though it had such asides on the "larger questions" as this: "If people in their homes could feel those feelings for an hour or even just know about them, I think we would be an inch or two closer to winning the war and trying like hell to make the peace permanent." Hersey balanced such a statement earlier in the book when he wrote that the Marines fought, above all, to "get this goddam thing over and get home."

Hersey stayed a month on Guadalcanal and never afterward spent any more time with a particular military unit than he did with the Marine company at the three-day battle of the Matanikau. He never again had as close and sustained a view of combat, although he would spend many hours interviewing such survivors of combat as Lieutenant John F. Kennedy. He lacked the intensive exposure of correspondents Richard Tregaskis or Ernie Pyle. But he was given a spectacular view of the war.

He went from the Solomons to Sicily and later to Russia. He interviewed men from all the American fighting services and most of the special fields within each service. He met a great assortment of the war's civilian victims. He reported occupation, liberation, and rehabilitation. *Time* and *Life* also gave him solemn duties that most other reporters were fortunate to avoid: his beats occasionally included morale and war aims. At the same time that he wrote about the Matanikau battle, he filed a story about the Marines on Guadalcanal, sections of which could have been run with the Nash-Kelvinator ad: "As a fighter, he is a cross between Geronimo, Buck Rogers, Sergeant York, and a clumsy, heartsick boy." For *Life*'s Christmas number in 1943, Hersey wrote a text to accompany reproductions of paintings by the magazine's overseas artists. Titled "Experience by Battle," the article is a curious mixture of statements. He mentions hatred of the Japanese enemy: "call it neurosis, call it hatred that consumes men and never leaves them, call it whatever you wish, the feeling of men who have fought the Japanese is permanent and terrible." The future author of *Hiroshima* and *The War Lover* also wrote: "The war will end sooner for aviators, and their scars will heal quicker, if they can concentrate on hitting the enemy carefully and well." A few pages later, he wrote:

> For American soldiers, who know their duty when they see it but who love life so very much, the Japanese warrier code is beginning to be a thing of pity. It says "Duty is weightier than a mountain, while death is lighter than a feather." The Marines who fought on Guadalcanal wanted only to live to fight victoriously another day and after the fight, to be happy and relaxed and American for many other days.

This observation lying so close to the real questions of life and death in wartime faintly anticipates what he would write years later about survival and tenacity, but in 1943 and 1944 he was incapable of pursuing its implications.

Because World War II was fought more globally than the first, because news coverage had become more extensive and instantaneous, and because he worked for publications which exploited these new conditions in capsulating the news more effectively than their competitors, John Hersey had opportunities and handicaps given no earlier writer. He stood somewhere between the wire service editor in Oklahoma who wrote a novel about the Russian front from the leavings of his teletype and Norman Mailer, who was taking notes as a rifleman for a novel he was determined to write after the war.

A Bell for Adano is the sort of book one might expect Hersey to write at that time. He finished it within six weeks after he had filed a story for *Life* on the operations of the American military governor of Licata, Sicily. The article, which took up only two of *Life's* back pages, described a typical day at the desk of an unnamed American major, a New Yorker of Italian extraction. A merchant was told to compile a fair price list for food and clothing that had been impounded by the Fascists. A pretty girl was assured that her fiancé was a prisoner of war. Charges were dismissed in the case of a cart driver arrested for obstructing traffic. Hersey followed his training in observing these details, and then began his story in the spirit of his writing on war aims:

> For a long time we have taken pleasure in the difficulties met by Germany and Japan in organizing the conquered lands. Here at the major's desk you see difficulties, hundreds of them, but you see shrewd action, American idealism, and generosity bordering on sentimentality, the innate sympathy of common blood that so many

Americans have to offer over here. You see incredible Italian poverty, you see the habits of Fascism, you see a little duplicity and a
lot of simplicity and many things which are comic and tragic at one
time. Above all you see a thing succeeding and it looks like the
future.

This is a good precis of *A Bell for Adano*. When he turned to
write the novel, Hersey borrowed General Patton, contrived a
romantic interest for the major (provoking a lawsuit after the
war), and added the story of replacing the town bell. Everything
else is fictionalized journalism in the strictest sense. The point
of the first paragraph of the article is expanded and set in
italics as the foreword to the novel, and each case at the major's
desk is developed into an episode. *A Bell for Adano* was a huge
popular success. Even more than when he had written *Into the
Valley,* Hersey was praised in terms that made him a literary
90-day wonder. He was told that he had written "a magnificent
parable," and that, unlike the World War I cynics, he "could
look beyond both horror and heroics to the truth of what he had
seen." He "had everything needed to make a front-rank novelist,"
especially because of "his consuming interest in men and women
and his genuine love for them."

Hersey a modest man, could not accept these tributes as a
balanced critical estimate of his work. He understood better than
the reviewers of *A Bell for Adano* what effect the war had had
on his writing, and his understanding increased during his assignment in Moscow in 1944. There, while he was compelled to
report the war by listening to the salvos in Red Square proclaiming
the recapture of cities to the west, Hersey wrote an article for
the *Time* book section on the activity of Russian writers in
wartime. The section editor borrowed Gorki's phrase, "engineers of
the soul," for the title. "Not a word is written which is not a
weapon," Hersey observed, and he must have known of the old
Party slogan. The books of Sholokhov, Simonov, and others that
he had to summarize for his report he felt could not be criticized
in conventional terms. "The only fair test," Hersey wrote, "is to
see whether these writers have fulfilled their aims." He saw their
aims exactly as they saw them—nothing but to defeat the hated
enemy. The single determining fact about these Russian writers,
Hersey insisted, was that they had been in and out of the war.

Although more of a spectator than the Russians had been, as he
went in and out of the war, Hersey was more the war's product
than they were. To suggest what else influenced Sholokhov,

Simonov, and their colleagues in the war years is to ask if there could have a Soviet novel like *A Bell for Adano,* with a Soviet major standing up for a Hungarian cart driver against a Soviet general. Hersey had only the war as milieu and guide. Such assignments as writing notes under the heading of "Experience by Battle" and producing a book on Bataan a month after the surrender of Corregidor strained Hersey as much as Russian writers had been strained in using words as weapons. While his wartime books must be judged honestly by standards applied to other American book printed in 1942 and 1944—Saul Bellow's *Dangling Man,* for example—they must also be judged by their aims for the same extenuation that Hersey sought for the Russians. When he had the opportunity to study how men survived their ordeals, as he did at the Matanikau and when he interviewed Lieutenant Kennedy, Hersey helped himself become a novelist. Otherwise, on V-E Day, when he won his Pulitzer Prize, Hersey was a man who had had to write too much too soon.

Then came *Hiroshima* for which Hersey had more time for an assignment than he had ever been given before—and a subject without precedent. Not just because it appeared in *The New Yorker,* instead of in *Time* or *Life,* this reporting is stripped of any overt pleas for disarmament and international cooperation. Paradoxically, as Hersey was becoming a better reporter than he had been for the Luce publications, he was also preparing to write a far greater novel than *A Bell for Adano.*

He first knew that he would write the novel which became *The Wall* when he toured the sites of German atrocities in Eastern Europe shortly after they had been uncovered by the Red Army. The fact that there were survivors on hand to interview struck him even more than the horrors themselves. He saw what he called "evidence that mankind was indestructible" at the same time that he saw evidence of previously unimaginable genocide. His months in Hiroshima later, as he said, "lent urgency to what had been a vague idea."

In 1947 he talked with survivors of Auschwitz, particularly with one man who had struggled and connived to become a *kapo*—a camp official. This unnerving experience, which he withheld from print until 1963, when it was published in *Here to Stay: Studies in Human Tenacity,* led him to write instead about the ghetto survivors who had lived as families and communities up to the end. When he began work on this, he soon learned that there existed a flood of diaries, organization records, statistics, medical histories, and songs about the Warsaw ghetto, and that very little of all this would ever be translated. Undertaking to read what he could, he also engaged two translators to read from the original Polish and Yiddish onto a wire recorder in rapid English. Most of his time for the next several months was spent listening to these recordings. They changed all his plans and reversed his established habits of approaching materials. His translators had relatives who had died in the ghetto, and their sight translating turned them into involuntary story-tellers as they began to skip, summarize, and add their own impassioned comments on the documents. The process gave Hersey the illusion of felt experience, instead of seeing a documentary—exactly the reverse of the information-gleaning for *Men on Bataan*. As a result he decided, tentatively, to shape his novel as a series of first-person narratives, but he kept on listening, and by the time his translators were through, they had given him a million recorded words. It was late 1948 and he was still not ready to begin writing. He took notes on his notes, "as if," he said, "I were interviewing the three of us—the two translators and myself." He thought of seeking out actual ghetto survivors, but decided that the translations had brought him close enough to events while still permitting him to create his own characters.

He performed several routine chores such as devising a ghetto chronology and a list of nineteen themes. The first of these themes was, "In danger, some men surprised into heroism; others amazed to find themselves corrupt." Theme number eighteen was "The Wall." A few characters began sticking out from a list of fifty; among them, Noach Levinson, who was changing from a *Judenrat* official to "a kind of intuitive historian," whose comments would be inserted between the other characters' narratives.

After a year and a half of preliminary work, Hersey had come with a plan he thought final. Then, four-fifths of the way through a longhand draft, he realized that Noach Levinson's choruses were becoming too long to squeeze into their assigned spaces, and that Levinson, with the help of the story-tellers on the wire-recorder, had taken over the novel. Hersey then made a frightening decision for a journalist-turned-novelist. "This particular story needed to be told with an authority my gifts could not evoke," he wrote. "It needed to be told by a participant in the events; and my creature, Levinson, some of whose literary mannerisms, I confess, were annoying, did seem to me to have the gifts, the background, and above all the experience to make his story believed." Thus, the novel took shape as "the Levinson archive," the jottings of a fictional hero who enters the story as a scholarly isolate and leaves as a child of a family of survivors.

When he had finished writing *The Wall,* Hersey could accurately if modestly speak of himself as a novelist of contemporary history. Complexities beyond a reporter's grasp were breached in the writing of this novel. Through his reading, through taking notes on his notes, and through that process by which he became captive of his translators and creator of Noach Levinson, he wrote a novel which goes beyond recording its day to affirm that survival from the ghetto was an instance of a universal theme. How far he had come from the prologue to *A Bell for Adano* and how surprising that he had also advanced beyond the "inspired journalism" of *Hiroshima!*

Not all of his subsequent fiction consists of such exemplary novels of contemporary history. The five later books differ in content and in form as much as any five books by any of Hersey's contemporaries. He remains outside the ranks of acceptable subject for the growing criticism of postwar American fiction. He is excluded because he is or was a journalist. Sometimes it is said flatly that he is not a novelist. He is a little like John Dos Passos, who is so difficult to pin down as a novelist or a reporter or an historian that we may all come to accept his own definition of his works as "contemporary chronicles." Both Hersey and Dos Passos might be called "writers." Unfortunately, we seem to have no such sweeping term.

"The Strenuous Life" as a Theme in American Cultural History

Edwin H. Cady

The first problem with the theme of the strenuous life in America is that the word "theme" is an evasion. A set of cultural factors is complex in the extreme; "theme" is used here precisely because it is a word elastic and inexact enough to cover a multitude of related but disparate meanings.

Second, I am none too sure about the adequacy of the Theodore Rooseveltian phrase, "the strenuous life," as a name for the set of phenomena concerned. Clearly it is a mixed as well as multitudinous thing in our culture: overt and covert, playful, ritual, profoundly motivational as well as expressive, so extraordinarily broad and frequent in its appeal as to seem more nearly a universal than any other complex I can think of, incredibly Protean and its forms.

I got into consideration of the theme of the strenuous life by trying to make sense to myself of Stephen Crane's well-known attitudes toward life as war, toward the problems of fate, courage, and irony, and toward the experience of athletics which he, apparently uniquely among major American authors, had undergone, enjoyed, and exploited. Working at all that, I began to see that the trope of "The Game" was far less trivial to the American imagination than had been supposed and that Crane's power derived in major part from his laying vital hold on a major American phenomenon.

What is that phenomenon? For lack of adequate definition, let us try to come at it by way of some famous quotations. The first is that Rooseveltian *locus classicus,* easy to parallel from his writings but in this case no doubt very significantly addressed to an audience of Chicago tycoons by a speaker at the height of his military and pre-Presidential fame. The essence of what Roosevelt said was:

> . . . I wish to preach, not the doctrine of ignoble ease, but the doctrine of the strenuous life, the life of toil and effort, of labor and strife; to preach that highest form of success which comes . . . to the man who does not shrink from danger, from hardship, or from bitter toil . . .

No one will be surprised to remember that this Rooseveltian challenge found echoes in the expression, as it obviously did in the life-style, of John Fitzgerald Kennedy. Here is that President who was somehow uniquely contemporaneous to us defending the breathtaking American investment in exploration of space. With a typical sense of historical perspective, Kennedy got into his subject by saying to his audience at Rice University:

> William Bradford, speaking in 1630 of the founding of the Plymouth Bay Colony, said that all great and honorable actions are accompanied with great difficulties, and both must be enterprised and overcome with answerable courage. . . . We set sail on this new sea because there is new knowledge to be gained, and new rights to be won, and they must be won and used for the progress of all people. . . . But why, some say, the moon? Why choose this as our goal? And they may well ask why climb the highest mountain. Why, 35 years ago, fly the Atlantic? Why does Rice play Texas?
>
> We choose to go to the moon. We choose to go to the moon in this decade and do the other things not because they are easy, but because they are hard, because that goal will serve to organize and measure the best of our energies and skills. . . .

Kennedy did well to pick up from Bradford not, be it observed, the note of Puritan zeal but the Renaissance gentlemen's note of magnamimity: great-heartedness. The strenuous theme springs from the earliest roots of the American experience: exploring and colonizing adventurousness; Puritan, Quaker and otherwise Utopian and "come-outer" zeal; the confident patience of the builders of culture and the hot egotism of gamblers; frontier toughness; the faith, vision, defiance, yet balance of the founders of the Republic. The centrality of this notion is as old as it is new. There is nothing in the least superficial, external, merely popular or merely muscular and vulgar, certainly nothing trivial about the influence and significance of the theme.

One might pick it up in Edwards and Woolman as well as Franklin, in Washington, Adams, Jefferson—or Hamilton and Paine, Freneau and Fisher Ames. It is not merely Jacksonian but Emersonian—and Hawthornian, Melvillean and Thoreauvian as well as Whitmanian. The ringing quotations from a romantic age which illustrate its esteem for strenuosity were answered in the post-Civil War Gilded Age with expressions of ambivalent doubt and disillusion. Yet in the long run Howells and Twain and James— like DeForest and Cable and Garland—kept faith in an ultimacy of moral heroism more important than any other consideration. Of Stephen Crane we need say no more; and the case of Henry Adams in this connection should be obvious.

William James may have been speaking, far from trivially, for the minds of Americans of his own time and since in the essay "The Moral Philosopher and the Moral Life" which makes a part of *The Will to Believe:*

> The deepest difference, practically, in the moral life of man is . . . between the easy-going and the strenuous mood. When in the easy-going mood the shrinking from present ill is our ruling consideration . . .
>
> When, however, we believe that a God is there, and that he is one of the claimants, the infinite perspective opens out. . . . The more imperative ideals now begin to speak with an altogether new objectivity and significance, and to utter the penetrating, shattering, tragically challenging note of appeal. They ring out like the call of Victor Hugo's alpine eagle . . . and the strenuous mood awakens at the sound. It sayeth among the trumpets, Ha! ha! it smelleth the battle afar off, the thunder of the captains and the shouting. . . . All through history, in the periodical conflicts of puritanism with the don't care temper, we see the antagonism of the strenuous and genial moods, and the contrast between the ethics of infinite and mysterious obligation from on high, and those of prudence and the satisfaction of merely finite need.
>
> The capacity of the strenuous mood lies so deep down among our natural human possibilities that even if there were no metaphysical or traditional grounds for believing in God, man would postulate one simply as a pretext for living hard, and getting out of the game of existence its keenest possibilities of zest.

Let us illustrate something of the kaleidoscopic variety of the cultural configurations of our theme. But perhaps the safest to put forward first is the familiar matter of nature and "Naturism," with its involvements in the problems of the savage and the primitive, the agrarian; the rivalry of the country, the village, the town, and the city; and the modern terrors of urban-adaptivity and the concrete jungle. Here, too, are much involved the questions of civilization, its humanities and its discontents; the lovely theme of life in the open—walking, climbing, canoeing, and living with the wilderness; loving landscape, feeling one's way into it by intuition, instinct, the perception of "correspondences," or even that mystical process of projection and identification which makes one become like "a transparent eyeball in nature." We may associate here the ideas of the Frontier and the West as well as the modern concern for the conservation of nature as a duty to social good and to the future.

It is not too hard a transition to go from that universe of discourse to another which examines the strenuous animal who inhabits nature and which, orienting his strenuosity, examines particularly the theme of American *masculinity*. Even as in preliterate societies, in our culture masculinity is closely bound to certain *rites de passage*, having to do with matters of initiation, the open road, danger, test, courage, discipline, and with learning, as we say, "to pay the price." For we remain, as we have always been, much concerned with struggle, competition, survival, and success. We remember the wilderness arts of the frontier and pioneering and associate them with "free enterprise" and "the rugged individual," with an ideal of democracy as competition free and fair, and with worries about exploiting people and idolatry of "the bitch-goddess Success." We assimilate, sometimes oddly, to all this certain ideals of the American gentleman, his chivalry, generosity, and responsibility; ideals of heroes, hero-worship and "the happy warrior"; and a rather unstable notion of "physical fitness."

In the forefront of observation about American masculinity always has been a registration of certain tensions between masculine and feminine. We have considered long over questions of masculine identity, boyhood and boy-life, sexual identity and "machismo" —that Latin something for which we have no word. Closely related are the much-bruited but still obscure tensions between masculine vice—the life-styles of the barracks, the gym, the gambling hall, the brothel—and that dim and shape-shifting puzzle we label with a most abused tag, "the genteel tradition." Though there are of course traditions of the genteel strenuous, the opposition would seem to have had all the best (or worst?) of it. There are weighty attractions in masculine humor—the vernacular and profane as against bourgeois and genteel talk, the practical joke and dirty story, the deflating and leveling powers of folk and frontier satire and burlesque. And what shall stand against the attractions of violence? There are the good old traditions of the fight: wrestling, fist-fighting, rough-and-tumble, "no holds barred"—bite, stomp and gouge. And, with weaponry, the *code duello* degenerating into "shoot on sight," feuding, bushwhacking. These are ancient modes now largely honored in the breach except in the ritual South. Now we have advanced to such refinements of manliness as the rumble, the mugging, the gratuitous assault and murder.

Once again, no doubt a negotiable transition can be traced from all of that to the obviously strenuous themes of *war and combat.* Here in addition to the subjects of the nation's relations to its militia, national guard, and professional armed services fall the American themes of war and peace together with the query: is there an American way in war? Also, what about our expansionist sentiments—Young America, Manifest Destiny, Imperialism, the Pax Americana? And, finally, the more pressing question: is there a moral equivalent to war and, if so, can we find and institutionalize it in time?

Absorbing as all these aspects of our theme are, the closest to the heart of the matter is a final natural grouping: sports and their American evolution, or to subsume the entire topic under one reverberating title, "The Game." Strenuosity can be charming in the guise of a free sportive discharge of excess energy. The creative spontaneity of *homo ludens* is one of man's more hopeful and attractive moods. It links him with all the powers which like Robert Frost's "West Running Brook" force life up against the streams of entropy running down to cold oblivion in nature. These are forces of sex, procreativity, higher organization, differentiation, love, and altruism. They link the best we know of man to the blind, cheerful, gratuitous adventurousness of protoplasm.

So The Game, sport and play, is not mere childish, trivial, disinterested or insignificant horsing around. It is not merely the inconsequential ego-exercise of vulgar gambling. Frost, whose work would richly repay analysis in terms of "the strenuous life," makes the point elegantly in the final lines of "Two Tramps in Mud Time":

> Only where love and need are one
> And the work is play for mortal stakes,
> Is the deed ever really done
> For Heaven and the future's sakes.

American culture is of course a living branch of European or "Western" culture. And the most cursory perspective of that culture reveals a striking evolution. From earliest historic times, sport in Western culture was reserved for "persons"—elite persons, aristocrats, that is—and in large part denied to subelite, and especially to peasant, nonpersons. Sport was therefore a badge and a shaping determinant of values, of value in persons, and indeed of individuality. There was a longish middle period where, especially in Britain and therefore here, sport and personhood broadened down. Now, in the democratized, industrialized, and (at least theoretically) personalized modern world, sport is everywhere increasingly a passion.

Why? A quick answer would seem to involve two essential factors. First, Western culture, like most historical culture, has been overwhelmingly a gambling culture—one where competition, risk-taking, and the ego-satisfactions of victory have predominated. And insofar as the rest of the world has looked to become "modern" through industrialization, it has been converted far more efficiently to gambling than to, for instance, Christianity. No doubt we missionize the one gospel more powerfully than the other.

Second, sport is a peculiarly expressive and impressive sort of ritual. That is why it has become an increasingly effective, appealing mode of international communication. As ritual, sport offers intense emotional participation and focus directly to competitors and vicariously to audiences. Quite aside from the equally intense private, psychic and physiological factors, in its public aspects sport as ritual offers the satisfactions of community, of clear abstraction within formal bounds and limitations, and the immediateness of speedy resolution. Encapsulating man's fate in a gambling culture, it offers him swiftness and perfection in victory with safe prospects for tomorrow and the next time in defeat. It supplies heroes and celebrity for the love of glory. It holds out symbols of courage, pride, and excellence, of the tragic sense of life, of sacrifice and disinterestedness. No wonder artists of every sort feel close to athletes and their sports.

Therefore the thorough student of American culture must understand hunting, fishing, mountaineering, and life in the wild. He must know the evolutions of our games and athletes and especially of our intercollegiate games and patterns of competition. He must study sporting subcultures and popular involvement, sportsmanship, the amateur, the mucker, and professionalism with its contradictory hold on the traditions of "show-biz" and of "the old pro." He will get involved with such phenomena as "muscular Christianity" and the interrelations of sport with democracy.

Sport offers not only ritual and symbol but a social binder and a door, an upward way, of social mobility opening for the ethnically and racially suppressed—for the "hungry boy" who is anxious to "pay the price" and win the prize. On the other hand, sport is not infrequently a divider of the elite from the vulgar.

There always have been sporting snobbery, sporting conspicuous waste, the steady flight, now at jet speed, from the "Out" to the "In." Thus sport is aboriginally entangled with popular culture, national institutions, the very language. Phenomena surrounding "the fan" remain rich in mystery. And last there are the evolution of sporting journalism and of its uniquely specialized artist, the sports writer.

Another enlightening way to approach the topic is through *significant figures*—archetypes, artists, authors, popularists, and theorists. One convenient if not strictly accurate way to distinguish among these is to segregate historical figures from "myths and modes"—somewhat riskily taking the former to represent a kind of objective reality denied the latter. Some "myths and modes": the wilderness hunter, the leatherstocking, the frontiersman, the Indian-hater, the "White Indian," the river man, the mountain man, the guide, the pioneer woman, the steamboat man: pilot, captain, roustabout, the "canawler," the Mormon, the sodbuster, the naturalist, the woman athlete, the Gibson Girl, the whaler, the explorer, the logger, the "sporting woman" the filibusterer, the railroader, real and synthetic folk heroes (the sort with names), the cowboy, dime novel, horse opera, space opera, the jingo, Frank Merriwell, Stover at Yale, Notre Dame and the Four Horsemen, the foreign or war correspondent, the suffragette, the highjacker, "the Conservative," "The era of wonderful nonsense," the champ, "the old pro" and "the busher."

A list of notably illustrative names of "actual" persons might include, in addition to those already mentioned: John Smith, Miles Standish, John Winthrop, Roger Williams; Boone, Kenton, and Weiser; Fenimore Cooper, Parkman, Audubon; Mike Fink, Crockett, Bowie, Carson; Andrew Jackson, Benton, Fremont; Theodore Winthrop, T. W. Higginson, Sidney Lanier; any of a dozen sets of Civil War personalities; Rockefeller, Carnegie, Fisk, Diamond Jim Brady; Clarence King, J. W. Powell, Buffalo Bill; all the Darwinists; Homer, Eakins, Ryder, Bellows, Remington, Wister, Zane Grey; R. H. Davis, Frank Norris, Jack London; Burroughs, Muir, Seton; Camp, Muldoon, Heffelfinger, Honus Wagner, Jack Johnson, Billy Sunday; Alger and Stratemeyer, MacArthur and Hemingway, Rickard and Mizener, Colonel Biddle and Ring Lardner; Rice, Pegler, Brown, Kieran; S. E. White, E. R. Burroughs, Upton Sinclair, Owen Johnson; Wolfe, Faulkner, Warren; Gompers, Haywood, Hillquit, Debs, Lewis, Reuther; FDR, Truman, "Ike," LBJ; industrial and financial giants by the score;

William White, Bunche, King, Farmer; . . . . Ezra Pound . . . . Cassius Clay . . . . Ayn Rand . . . . Anyone could add others at least equally good.

These lists are neither exhaustive nor intended to be anything but suggestive—like the whole paper. But they may suggest that the theme of the "strenuous life" in America is a lode richly worth mining.

The Juvenile Approach to American Culture, 1870-1930

Russel B. Nye

The belief that books may be used as tools for instilling virtue in the young is an old and honored one. Since ancient times literature (using the term loosely) has served as a medium for instructing youth in the manners and morals of society, and for introducing them to the major problems of adult life. The books young people read, therefore, often provide reflections of what society assumes to be valuable, and of the standards it holds. Certainly in America, where the Calvinistic heritage and the popularity of the sentimental-didactic novel combined justify it, a juvenile literature which amused, taught, and exhorted needed no encouragement.

While it is not the purpose here to trace the source of such literature in the United States from its beginnings, it ought to be pointed out that by the close of the eighteenth century there was a thriving market for books whose purpose was to introduce young people to their culture and to provide them with minimal equipment to fit into it—books such as the Reverend Thomas Day's British classic, *Sandford and Merton* (1783-89), still being reprinted 125 years later, or the popular American equivalent, the Reverend Enos Hitchcock's *Farmer's Friend* (1793). These and other books like them were hardy perennials, given as Sunday-school prizes or by doting aunts, grimly didactic, primly moralistic, and no doubt fearsomely dull to children. Yet what they taught —piety, work, thrift, self-sacrifice, humility—represented deeply-held and unanimously respected American virtues. Such books, a nineteenth-century reviewer wrote quite correctly, formed "an instrument of immense power in education and civilization," with "a serious responsibility to form a correct public taste."[1]

What radically changed the character of American juvenile fiction in the early nineteenth century was its discovery of the frontier and the Indian. The captivity and pioneer tales of the previous century, as they emerged from the treatment administered by Cooper, Simms, Bird, and others, contributed a new kind of literary subject matter to the juvenile market. What Cooper did for adult readers, Joseph Holt Ingraham did at a lower level, creating blood-and-thunder western and pirate tales in their full glory. Ingraham, one might easily argue, with his sure sense of the cliché, his acute use of the sensational, and his barbarously Gothic style, was the grandfather of the dime novel.

It is with the dime novel, of course, that this paper really begins, and the dime novel begins with the publishing house of Beadle and Adams, formed in 1856 by the Beadle brothers and a young Irishman, Robert Adams.[2] The company did not do well until in 1860 (the year of Ingraham's death) it published a paperbound novel which sold for ten cents, titled *Malaeska; The Indian Wife of The White Hunter,* followed shortly by an even greater success, *Seth Jones; or The Captives of the Frontier.* Beadle and Adams opened the floodgates, and for the next forty years these dime books, (later reduced to a nickel) poured from the presses by tons. Their innovation was not one of kind or content, but one of production and merchandising; what the House of Beadle did was to put 70,000 words into a yellow paper cover with a lurid drawing on it and sell it for a dime. Erasmus Beadle, the P. T. Barnum of the early juvenile trade, simply applied big business methods to publishing. His aim, he said, was to "see how much I could give for ten cents; cash sales, no credit," and he retired with a fortune of over three millions.

The best of the Beadle novels hardly attained the level of mediocrity by any reasonable standards, but they were highly conventional in their regard for contemporary standards of conduct. The action might be bloody and the heroes rough-hewn, but the books were resolutely virtuous. Early dime-novel characters never smoked, drank, cursed, or gambled, and they always won over characters who did. Erasmus Beadle's regulations forbade "all things offensive to good taste . . ., subjects of characters that carry an unmoral taint . . ., and what cannot be read with satisfaction by every rightminded person, old and young alike."[3] What parents objected to in the dime-novels was not their morality, but their emphasis on sensationalism, violence, and overwrought emotionalism, especially as the type began to degenerate in the seventies and eighties. The demand for increasing suspense and action pushed authors closer to absurdity; the quality of the writing, never high, slipped into the worst kind of shoddy prose. At first the writers drew heroes more or less from real life—Buffalo Bill, Daniel Boone, Texas Jack, Kit Carson, Big Foot Wallace, and so on—but when they ran out of material they soon invented wildly improbable characters of the order of Deadwood Dick, Deadshot Dave, Rattlesnake Ned, or the Black Avenger. Within a few decades the stories were out of hand, filled with a disrespect for law and the proprieties that led to the canonization of train-robbers, outlaws, and criminals such as Jesse James, the Youngers, Billy the Kid, and their fictional counterparts.

But what was of more importance, the Indian-killing, train-robbing violence of the paper shockers had begun by the eighties to lose its relevance to postwar American society. Even in their most popular period, the dime novels found their market deeply cut by a new kind of story, better fitted to the times—Horatio Alger's stories of poor boys who succeeded in business, of country boys who (like Dick Whittington) confronted and conquered the city, boys bound to rise to fame and fortune—stories related much more directly to the ideals and aspirations of changing American society. Alger helped to provide boys with something the dime novels could not, and which the young American badly needed; that is, some grasp of the changes in nineteenth-century social and economic values, some understanding of the new forces of contemporary society and how to control them.

A number of aspects of Alger's work need to be discussed at length, but this consideration will be limited to a brief consideration of four: his continuation of the traditional American theme of self-help and self-reliance; his services as instructor to his era in the complexities of a new kind of economic society; his interpretation of the social values of the middle-class virtues; and his recognition of the changed nature of American urban life. In these ways, certainly, Alger caught the meaning of what had been taking place in the postwar United States, and served the youth of the country well by explaining it in understandable terms. What Alger did, in effect, was to exemplify in his books many of the prevailing concepts of what American life was like, and how some of the traditional American beliefs functioned within it.

First of all, Alger's books reinforced the ingrained American faith in the virtues of personal independence and self-reliance. He restated what Franklin told his age, and what Emerson, in somewhat more exalted terms, told his. In an era of urbanization and industrialization, undergoing a real but unnoticed population explosion, the individual was in danger of submerging himself in a swiftly developing mass society. Alger's boy-heroes reaffirmed in highly satisfactory terms all the old values of Puritan and Franklinian individualism.[4]

The standard Alger plot concerns a boy of fifteen or so, usually fatherless, who has to make his own way, often in the city, against heavy financial and social odds. Sometimes he has to support a widowed mother, tormented by the village squire who holds a mortgage on her little cottage or scrabble farm. Whatever the circumstances, the boy has to stand on his own two feet and face the practical problem of getting on in the world and finding a place in it. The titles of the Alger books play variations on this theme of self-reliance—*Work and Win, Strive and Succeed, Facing the World, Do and Dare, Adrift in New York, Struggling Upward, Striving for Fortune, Making His Way, Try and Trust, Sink or Swim, Risen from the Ranks.*

We know from the first few pages exactly what obstacles the boy faces, and the excitement of the narrative (such as it is) lies in how he comes to grips with his world and subdues it. Alger usually explains in scrupulously precise terms what these problems are. In *Do and Dare,* for example, the young hero's mother, the village postmistress, made exactly $398.50 the preceding year. Her mortgage, held by the rascally squire, is $481 at about 8 per cent; she owes him on instalment plus interest. Thus the reader can figure for himself, when young Tom, Jack, Luke, Ben, Andy, or Dick gets a clerking job at $3 a week and contracts also to tutor the rich man's son in Latin, exactly how much progress he can make toward making that payment on time. What it takes for the boy to succeed, of course, are piety, courage, thrift, alertness, punctuality, morality, hard work, and the rest of the constellation of virtues surrounding self-reliance. "Have you got grit?" his employer asks the young hero of *Strive and Succeed.* "Do you generally succeed in what you undertake? Grit weighs heavily in this world." Alger's plots presented a simplified version of the great and abiding American belief in the ultimate success of individual effort; and whatever his shortcomings as a writer, which were many and grievous, he presented it with tremendous effectiveness to his generation.

Second, Alger's books provided boys with their first intelligible picture of contemporary economic life. His was the era of American business expansion, when businessmen worked hard, took daring risks, built giant corporations and amassed incredible fortunes. One must not forget that Russell Conwell's famous lecture, "Acres of Diamonds," repeated hundreds of times during these years, exhorted its listeners, "Get rich! Get rich! I say you have no right to be poor!" This was the age of Rockefeller, Carnegie, Vanderbilt, Guggenheim, Harriman, Gould, Fisk, and other multiple millionaires to whom riches came so suddenly and in such profusion that simply how to control wealth became one of the pressing ethical, political, and social problems of the time. Alger knew this, and the majority of his books deal with questions raised by money—how one gets it, what one does with it, what happens when one does not have it. To Alger the pursuit of wealth could be challenging, exciting, and satisfying, as indeed it was to his generation, and his hero's progress toward his first million was the thread which held the majority of Alger's plots together. In the background of Alger's books was the story of Carnegie's rise from bobbin-boy to steel king, of Buck Duke selling tobacco on the road, of Edison hawking papers on Michigan trains. Alger's books were made real to his readers by life itself, for they embodied the great American dream that any right-thinking and right-acting American boy could by *Struggling Upward* succeed in *Finding a Fortune.*

How did one get rich in Alger's books? Here the legend is at variance with the facts. The Alger hero is honest, manly, cheerful, intelligent, self-reliant, ambitious, moral, frugal, and all else that he need be, but it is not by reason of any of these attributes, admirable as they are, that he becomes rich. The fact is that wealth in Alger comes by reason of the lucky break, by seizure of the chance opportunity. Ragged Dick saves his pennies, but when he rescues a child from the river her father turns out to be a rich banker who gives Dick a job. Phil the Fiddler, ground under the padrone system, falls exhausted in a snowstorm at the door of a wealthy old physician who has lost a son of Phil's age. Tom Thatcher catches a runaway horse, and in the buggy is the golden-haired daughter of a wealthy Wall Street broker. Sam, in *Sam's Chance,* finds a gold nugget approximately the size of a basketball; the hero of *Bound to Rise* befriends a lonely old man who gives him a sizable packet of downtown Tacoma real estate. Worthless mining stock in Alger stories always turns out to be worth hundreds of thousands; wealthy merchants, saved from robbery by the young heroes, invariably give them good jobs and rich rewards.

Frank the Cash Boy saves his meager salary, but he is really set on his way to wealth by capturing a thief; Alger remarks, "It is precisely to such lucky chances that men are often indebted for their advancement." An acute observer of the life around him, Alger knew better than to make wealth a matter of either luck or work alone; to him success was made out of labor plus the breaks, of ability plus the opportunity to capitalize on it.

Alger's boys are such model youths, and they save their money so carefully, that the modern reader is likely to miss the point. His message is not that you can save a great deal of money on a small salary, or that you ought to chase runaway buggies. The lesson is that money will come to him who is able to capitalize on the lucky opportunity—work and save, but watch for the break that may come only once to any man. In effect, one may say with some reason that the real heroes of the books are not the bootblacks and newsboys and store clerks, but the rich bankers, merchants, and stockbrokers who have seized their chances, and whom these boys hope to emulate. Alger made a clear distinction among rich men. There were smalltown, minor-league rich men who foreclosed mortgages, dispossessed widows, and threatened young men with ruin. (One of the really satisfying scenes in an Alger book is the confrontation scene, when the young hero returns, his wallet stuffed with greenbacks and sporting a gold watchchain, to pay off the mortgage to the grasping squire just as it falls due.) There were useless rich men, snobbish, idle parasites who, like Augustus Fitz-Herbert in Alger's poem, *Nothing to Do,*

> . . . cherishes deep and befitting disdain,
> For those who don't live in the Fifth Avenue,
> As entirely unworthy the notice of thought,
> Of the heir of two millions and nothing to do.

They are often represented in Alger by the rich boys who try every dirty trick in the book to win the big boat race, who fly into temper tantrums when foiled, and who are punished for their arrogance by a sudden plunge into poverty.[5] However, the good rich men in Alger are consistently kind, generous, and virtuous, and we know that Frank the Cash Boy or Mark Manning the Match Boy will be like them when he has made his millions. Alger perceived, as Carnegie did, the ethical values of the Gospel of Wealth and the responsibilities of Christian stewardship. The boys who read Alger set out to become richer and also better men, for Alger saw, as his age did, a relationship between virtue and wealth, money and morality, and he made this crystal clear to his readers.[6]

Alger's third contribution to an assessment of his times lay in his reaffirmation of the validity of American middle-class virtue. His books celebrated, in unmistakable terms, the values of individualism, self-reliance, and alertness to opportunity, and it was noticeable to his readers that success came to good boys, not bad ones. The old-fashioned virtues paid off in Alger's plots; it was not always exactly clear why, but they did, and the boy who was honest, punctual, respectable, and who honored his parents and his employer found success. The youth who grew up in the Alger tradition learned that work meant happiness, and that a busy life was a virtuous one, that it was best to stay out of debt and pay cash, that he who produced wealth was a useful citizen. As Alger wrote in one of his doggerel poems:

> Strive and Succeed, the world's temptations flee,
> Be Brave and Bold, and Strong and Steady be.
> Go Slow and Sure, and prosper then you must,
> With Fame and Fortune, while you Try and Trust.

Bound to Rise; or Up The Ladder (1873) is an excellent example of how Alger handled the relationship between success and virtue. He wrote in his introduction,

> Harry Walton and Luke Harris were two country boys who had the same opportunities to achieve success. Harry Walton by his efforts succeeded, and Luke Harris's life was a failure. Read this story and you will see what qualities in the one brought about his success, and what in the other caused his downfall.

Alger is not quite specific in detailing these qualities, but it is obvious by the end of the book that Harry succeeded by pursuing his education, paying his debts, dressing modestly, giving his best efforts to his job, and helping his indigent parents. Luke plays billiards, borrows more than he can repay, spends too much time on his clothes, and never reads a book. Harry continually revises his aims upward; Luke drifts, with apparently no aims at all.[7] When his break comes, Harry is ready for it and Luke is left far behind. The pattern is a familiar one in the Alger series, for Alger was constantly reassuring his readers that traditional virtues still meant something in the competitive, industrialized, urbanized society of the late nineteenth century. Alger had neither the intellectual equipment to formulate it, nor the literary skill to articulate it, but what he was trying to say was that there was a purposeful life and a pointless life, that there was a right way and a wrong way to live, and that the standards which determined them were still operative in times of great and unsettling change. Alger plots and Alger heroes gave the boys of the seventies and eighties an anchor to tie to in the era of Darwin, Sumner, Coxey, Ingersoll, Donnelly, Spencer, and the other movers and shakers of contemporary society.[8]

Fourth, Alger, almost alone among his fellow writers of juveniles, perceived the changing quality of city life and suggested how his readers might handle the problems it presented to the youth who had to make his way in it. He recognized the need of the city boy, or the country boy come to the city, for guidelines to lead him successfully into this new, dangerous, and frightening urban environment. The New York street urchins Alger knew, and the farm boys who streamed into the cities from the upstate hamlets, each determined to go from rags to riches as swiftly as possible, had little equipment with which to deal with the harsh facts of the city's life. Alger's view of it was fundamentally realistic; his books include thieves and sharpers, gangs, temptation and vice, drunkenness, cruelty, and the pitfalls of fashion and irresponsibility. They included also a good deal of practical information on living and working in the metropolis, on rooms, food, jobs, costs, recreation, and the like. This was the same kind of city that Jacob Riis and Stephen Crane and Theodore Dreiser and Jane Addams and the muckrakers saw, and Alger, in his minor way, gave his youthful readers information about how to cope with it.[9]

By the time of Alger's death in 1899, however, the popularity of the Alger strain in juvenile books was fast fading out. The things Alger boys strove for, the obstacles they faced, and the heroes they emulated were no longer the same. The rags-to-riches billionaire was becoming scarce; it took money to make money in 1900, and the sudden stroke of luck that might in 1870 take a poor boy from nothing to a million, now needed plenty of capital to take advantage of it. The legend of Alger persisted, but the opportunities for making great wealth were narrowing fast; a boy now needed technological skill, education, scientific talent, and highly-organized business know-how to struggle upward—not just energy, sobriety, and the rescue of the boss's daughter. Alger's theory, that opportunity lay open everywhere about, was obsolete, and American boys knew it. Juvenile readers were much more sophisticated in their attitudes toward social and economic values, and more familiar with city codes of behavior which had gradually ceased to hold terror for them.

There were also new publishing techniques, assembly-line authorship, and new sales tricks, as juvenile publishing became big business under the aegis of firms such as A. L. Burt, Street and Smith, Cupples and Leon, or Grosset and Dunlap. The Alger formula no longer filled the bill. Cleverer men than he were in the field, men who caught much more precisely and accurately the spirit of the times. Two of these were Gilbert M. Patten, who wrote under the name of "Burt L. Standish," and Edward Stratemeyer, who wrote under so many names that some of them are not yet known.

Patten, who already had experience in writing dime-novel shockers, in 1895 received an offer from Street and Smith to begin a series about a youngster at prep school, and Frank Merriwell, student at Fardale Academy, came into being the next year.[10] Patten produced 208 Merriwell books over the next twenty-odd years, detailing Frank's career at Fardale and Yale, his younger brother Dick's, and even part of Frank Junior's, to total sales of approximately 125 million copies. The Merriwell plots, whose details were familiar to an entire generation between 1900 and 1920, were frantically athletic. Frank won every big game in Fardale's history and Yale's, and so did Dick after him. Each was at Yale nine years, and each graduated with honors. Both were fullbacks, both were pitchers, both stroked the crew—Frank threw a "doubleshoot" ball that curved twice before it reached the plate, while Dick possessed a "jump ball" that rose a full foot as it approached the batter. In track meets the Merriwells ran the dashes, the half mile, the mile, did the pole vault, the broad jump, the high jump, and threw the hammer. In vacation periods they hunted big game, punched cows, explored the jungle, mined gold, and so on. Patten also, rather daringly, introduced girls into his stories, giving Frank two girl friends and Dick one.

In focusing his stories on school and college life and on athletics, Patten opened up for his young readers a world that Alger never knew. During the nineties, and especially after 1900, athletics turned professional. Baseball and football, though popular for half a century, became mass spectator sports and increasingly big business. Instead of the bankers and merchants of Alger's books, Patten's series reflected a boy's secret desire to be Home Run Baker, Christy Mathewson, Pudge Heffelfinger, or Three-finger Mordecai Brown. At the same time, this was also the era of

Theodore Roosevelt, the Boy Scouts, the outdoors of Ernest Thompson Seton, and "the strenuous life," when hunting, exploring, mining, ranching, and athletics were made to seem exciting and glamorous activities—even prize-fighting with its plug-uglies and gentlemen such as Sullivan, Corbett, Kilrain, and Ruby Robert Fitzsimmons. Patten caught the spirit of this emergent cult of mass sport in his books, tailoring them to the pattern of the new sets of heroes whom boys held in respect, and the new interests of a frenetically physical time.

The Merriwells tied morality and athletics together in highly satisfactory fashion. Patten, a pious man himself, felt that the series gave him "an opportunity to preach—by example—the doctrine of a clear mind in a clean and healthy body" and he took full advantage of it. "I did my best," he wrote later of his books, "to keep them clean, and make them beneficial without allowing them to become namby-pamby or Horatio Algerish." The Merriwells did not smoke, drink, or swear, because such habits were unhealthy and unathletic; thus Patten avoided the moral issue in his preaching and convinced his readers that morals and manliness went together. It is no wonder that parents who objected to the adventures of Rattlesnake Ned and Jesse James approved of the Merriwells.[11]

Implicit in the Merriwell books is a concept of success markedly different from that stated in Alger. The Alger hero's rise is measurable in accountable material terms; we know where our hero starts, where he will end, and we can measure his progress in the size of his wallet. The Merriwell books recognize success as something quite different, in terms of the personal satisfaction of excellence, of the assumption of authority through virtue, of establishing leadership by example, of excelling under the rules, of "doing the right thing" and "playing the game."[12]

As Alger equated wealth and virtue, so the Merriwells equated virtue with the discipline of sport—the books were intended, Patten said, "to fire a boy's ambition to become a good athlete, in order that he may develop into a strong, vigorous, and right-thinking man." Using the athletic contest as his central device, Patten stressed success as self-improvement, self-realization, self-control, self-conquest. "It is possible for every boy," Dick Merriwell once said, "to improve himself, to become handsomer, stronger, manlier." The Merriwells' morals are those of the game, their enemies' vices those allied to poor sportsmanship, lack of control, false ambition.[13] Villainy in the Merriwell world derived from evasion, distrust, hypocrisy, conceit, self-indulgence; virtue involved friendship, sincerity, frankness, true humility, regard for the rules. Chester Arlington, the villain of the Dick Merriwell series, although strong, handsome, athletic, and intelligent, has

> too much pride, too much conceit, too little sympathy with others, and too little undeviating honesty . . . Chester's one great weakness was that he could not recognize his own weak spots. He believed it impossible that he should fail through any fault of his own.

The Merriwells "play fair," a theme stressed in all the books; they "play fair with themselves, and the rest of the world," Patten's implied rule for living. Again using the analogy of the playing field, he emphasized the virtues of the competitor who refuses to give up and who plays the string out. In *Dick Merriwell's Grit* he inserted an eloquent passage about the "quitter" that might have come directly from Theodore Roosevelt himself:

> Do not quit. Above all things else, do not be a quitter. The boys who have a large amount of stick-to-it-iveness invariably develop into men who persist against all obstacles and succeed in the struggle of life. They rise above their companions and surroundings, and are pointed out as successful men. Those who do not see beneath the surface often say that their success is nothing but luck; of course there is a singular something called luck, but in nine cases out of ten luck plays little or no part in the game of life. . . . Quitters become ordinary men, followers of their more persistent and determined fellows. They form the rank and file of the laboring classes. They never rise to hold positions of trust and influence. At least, if one ever does rise through chance to hold such a position, it almost invariably happens that sometime his original weakness causes him to fail and fall. He is not a stayer.

Patten, like Alger, usually avoided the social issues of the day, but he allowed the Merriwells an occasional pointed comment. No Italians or Jews or Poles appear in the books—the Merriwell companions are Irish, English, Dutch, Scots, and so on—but on the other hand Frank once outraged a crowd by shaking hands with a Negro jockey who had ridden a good race, and the books never, like those of many of his contemporaries, used Negro or Jewish types for low comedy purposes.[14] Sports, in Patten's view, basing their rewards on ability and discipline, were democracy at work. Frank, when he tried out for Yale's baseball team, found that he was judged on his skill alone, leading him to realize that "In athletics strength and skill win, regardless of money or family; so it happened that the poorest man in the university stood a show of becoming the lion and idol of the whole body of young men . . ." a theme that Patten carried consistently through the series.

Neither Merriwell cared much for money; though the source of their income is always obscure, Frank is able to reply to an offer to hunt treasure in Peru, "I am so situated that the mere desire for riches might not be sufficient to induce me to participate in such a project." Noticeably, the young villains tend to be wealthy, idle, aristocratic young men, such as Roland Ditson, "a contemptible cur" whose parents "furnished him with plenty of loose change," and Chester Arlington, Dick's nemesis. Patten, in *Dick Merriwell's Choice,* gave his hero an eloquent passage about the meaning of wealth:

> "My friend," said Dick, "you're about old enough to learn the lesson that money doesn't make the man."
> "But money makes the mare go. Feller's got to have money to amount to anything in this world."
> "Not always. Some of the greatest men the world has ever known were poor men."
> "Don't believe it! Everybody is out for dough!"
> "Not everybody," said Dick. "Even in these modern times there are men who are too busy to make money. There are men who follow their profession or careers with a certain lofty purpose, and refuse to give over their object, even for a short time, in order that they may make money."

The shift of values since Alger's time was never made more evident, for such a speech could never come from Ragged Dick. The Merriwells speak to a different age and a different culture.

Though Patten's books sold spectacularly, Edward Stratemeyer's syndicate dominated the juvenile field for more than a quarter of a century until his death in 1930. Stratemeyer, a graduate of Street and Smith's writing stable, published the first three books about the famous Rover boys—Dick, Tom, and Sam, the fun-loving brother—in 1899, taking the Merriwells' adventures, adding a bit of Alger's morality, and creating an instantly successful series. In 1906 he took the Rover formula and added speed to make the Motor Boys series a runaway success, for the automobile was by then an accomplished fact and every boy dreamed of owning, as the Motor Boys did, a giant six-cylinder racer capable of forty miles an hour. Then Stratemeyer had an even better idea; he formed a syndicate and by 1908 he had at least ten juvenile series operating under ten different names, with a half-dozen or more hack writers working for him. Mass production had been known before in publishing. But Stratemeyer's assembly-line technique soon made him the Henry Ford of the juvenile industry.[15]

The Rover Boys and Motor Boys books, and the majority of other Stratemeyer productions, were built about adventure, action, humor, and suspense, with a minimum of instructive moralizing. Stratemeyer shrewdly recognized that what interested the general adult reading public would also interest youngsters, and so constructed his books that they fell just below the interest level of subnormal adult intelligence—that is, dealing with automobiles, airplanes, sports, westerns, sea and war stories, exploring, and so on. They were, in effect, watered-down popular pulps, geared to the adolescent mind. A mild and moral man himself, Stratemeyer never allowed violence to get out of hand; his heroes used their fists, hot water, whitewash, stout sticks, and various other weapons to defeat villains, but never guns.[16] Whether the books appeared under the name of "Arthur Winfield" (The Rovers), "Clarence Young" (The Motor Boys), "Captain Ralph Bonehill," "Frank V. Webster," "Roy Rockwood," "Jim Bowie," "Laura Lee Hope" (The famed Bobbsey Twins), "Carolyn Keene," "May Hollis Barton," or any other of the Stratemeyer pseudonyms, the formula remained that of the "action" pulp, diluted for youthful tastes.

The single exception, however, was the Tom Swift series, much of which was written under the name of "Victor Appleton" by Howard Garis, later successful as the creator of "Uncle Wiggly." Garis was a somewhat more resourceful writer than most of the Stratemeyer employees, and the Swift series was a distinct improvement over its companions, as well as the most popular syndicate property, since it sold 6½ million copies to the Rovers' six and the Motor Boys' four. There were forty Tom Swifts, published between 1910 and 1941, the last one eleven years after Stratemeyer died. Tom lives in Shipton, New York, and like his widowed father, is an inventor. His chum, Ned Newton, who works in a bank, is a fine, brave boy who serves as a kind of Boswell to Tom's genius. Feminine interest is supplied by Mary Nestor (whom Tom marries after a 31-year engagement) and humor by Mr. Damon, who stutters, Eradicate Simpson, a comic colored servant, and various dialect-speaking youngsters. Tom simply invents—almost everything one could think of—and the excitement of the plot lies in whether or not his invention will work, whether it can be protected from rival scientists or thieves, and whether it can be used to benefit one's friends, society or nation.

In Tom Swift, Stratemeyer and Garis hit on a formula shrewdly designed to catch the interest of boys who were growing up in the midst of the twentieth century's great burst of invention and technology. Machines are always magic to the adolescent male, and Tom, the most prolific and imaginative inventor of them all, gave his readers one major invention and at least six minor ones in each book. Garis and Stratemeyer simply took the adventure story of the Rovers, combined it with Jules Verne, Thomas Edison, Ford, Marconi, and all the others who contributed to the excitement of the machine age, and mixed into it the greatest assortment of gagets known to man.

The Swift books had the usual ingredients, a race, a chase, a capture, an escape, a few not very villainous villains, a decent respect for the properties. But what they had most of were machines—electric rifles, motorcycles, racing autos, various kinds of boats, television (in 1921), radios, eight different kinds of airplanes, guns, and a multitude of other things. Tom, in his private laboratory, casually solved problems that had stumped the world since Newton. What he invented was always *almost* plausible, just far enough around the corner to be visionary, not quite far enough to be absurd; many of his inventions, in fact, were only a year or so ahead of their real-life counterparts. A boy could read Tom Swift, a book at a time, feel that he was pretty well up on what was going on in science, and amaze his friends with bits of inaccurate but impressive scientific knowledge.[17]

It is this faith in science, this admiration for the machine, that set Tom Swift apart from the financially minded Algers, the hyperactive Merriwells, or the redoubtable Rovers, and made him a hero to the twentieth-century boy. Stratemeyer and Garis recognized the shift of values that took place in American society after 1900 and charted Tom's career accordingly. Alger's boys amassed fortunes by pluck and luck but, products of the Gilded Age that they were, to them material success seemed an end in itself. The athletic Merriwells, exponents of the ethics of the game, were proper heroes too, and the Rovers adventured in every part of the globe. Tom Swift had all of this and more. Though the books rarely mention money, Tom had $100,000 in the bank as early as 1914; he won dozens of races on land, sea, and in the air; he found adventures in tunnels, jungles, deserts, and at the bottom of the ocean and in the caves of ice. These were not the important things. What mattered was Tom's success at breaking through the barriers of the unknown. His books were filled, in their naive way, with the excitement of a conquest of matter and space, the thrill of accomplishing with one's own brain and hands what others had hoped to do. It was not Rockefeller or Carnegie, Honus Wagner or Eddie Plank who were the implied heroes of the Swift books, but the Wright brothers, Steinmetz, Tesla, Edison, and the others who were pushing back the frontiers of knowledge and invention. Whereas Alger's boys faced the problems of an urbanized, acquisitive society, and the Merriwells the ethics of the competitive contest, Tom Swift grasped the technology of the machine age and brought it under control. He made scientific discovery exciting and technological advance adventurous, and most of all he made both seem useful and optimistic.

Even Tom could not go on forever. After Stratemeyer's death there was an obvious falling off in the quality of the series, and the last few were no more than weak science fiction. Furthermore, new heroes and new formulae appeared—Tarzan, Buck Rogers, the stylized and laundered dime-novel tradition in Gene Autry and Roy Rogers, then to Batman, Superman, and the end of the line, Mad Magazine. Most of all, there was nothing much left by 1940 for Tom to invent. The scientific developments of midcentury was simply too much for his home laboratory, which could hardly compete with Oak Ridge, jet flight, and the exploration of space. A victim of technological unemployment, Tom ended his career in a house-trailer, a sad anticlimax to the speedy motorcycles and giant planes of his youth.[18]

The Ragged Dicks of Alger, the Merriwell clan, and the Dave Dashaways and Baseball Joes of the Stratemeyer syndicate have all disappeared, but they still possess sentimental value for a balding generation who remember the pleasures of turning their peanut-butter-smeared pages in the attic on rainy days, or reading them by flashlight under the covers at night. They did no more harm, perhaps, than smoking cornsilk, and certainly the lessons they vaguely imprinted on the malleable minds of millions of long-gone adolescents were not bad ones. However, these books represent something more than nostalgia, for much of what they tried to express at their low but earnest level is still very much a part of the total cultural pattern; they still have something to tell the social historian. Whatever the hard facts of contemporary business life, the Alger legend of rags-to-riches by getting up early, sticking with it, and saving your pennies is very much with us. The American Schools and Colleges Association continues to make ten annual Horatio Alger awards to those leaders of American life who best exemplify dedication "to the free enterprise system and the American tradition of equal opportunity which enables a youth to overcome humble beginnings and achieve success through hard work, honesty, and determination." (Nothing is said of luck, unfortunately.) Alger, like Honest Abe and Poor Richard, has become part of American mythology. Each year at thousands of Downtown Coaches Associations, Kiwanis luncheons, and Alumni Club dinners, hundreds of athletic directors repeat the Merriwell message and quote Grantland Rice and Knute Rockne, while athletes of every kind endorse cereals, shave creams, and boys' clubs—though Gilbert Patten said it all best a half-century ago. Boys today find their heroes in astronauts and in their dreams ride into distant galaxies on thermocoupled inter-stellar drives, but behind them is the shadow of Tom Swift's challenge to the great unknowns of science. The values are still there; only the names and the means have changed.

Notes

1. William Everett, "Beadle's Dime Books," *North American Review,* XCIX (July 1864), 308.

2. For a complete account, see Albert Johannsen, *The House of Beadle and Adams* (Norman, Okla., 1950), and Edmund Pearson, *Dime Novels* (Boston, 1929).

3. William Everett, in 1864, found Beadle publications "without exception unobjectionable morally, whatever fault be found with their literary style and composition. They do not even obscurely pander to vice, or excite the passions." Everett, *op. cit.,* 308.

4. Irvin G. Wyllie, *The Self-made Man in America* (New Brunswick, 1954) is an excellent account of this tradition. The later nineteenth century abounded in self-help books such as William Makepeace Thayer's best-seller, *The Ethics of Success* (Boston, 1893-94); William Matthews' *Getting On In the World* (Chicago, 1883); C. H. Kent, *How To Achieve*

Success (New York, 1897), and of course Elbert Hubbard's famous *Message to Garcia,* published in 1899, the year of Alger's death. Alger, for that matter, was well aware of Franklin's example and the theme of the *Autobiography,* the poor boy who makes his way in the city, is an Alger favorite.

5. Alger had no illusions about what happened to you when you had money, and if you didn't. Tom Temple, in *Tom Temple's Career,* who finds that his friends simply reject him when he loses his estate, accepts it all realistically—"Tom had always understood that they cared for him only because he was rich, and he was neither astonished nor disappointed at the change." In *Brave and Bold,* when Halbert Davis falls on evil days, Alger writes, "The wealth and position upon which he had based his aristocratic pretension vanished, and in bitter mortification he found himself reduced to poverty. He could no longer flaunt his cane and promenade the streets in kid gloves, and he was glad to accept a position in the factory store, where he was compelled to dress according to his work." Alger was extremely conscious of the symbols of wealth and what they meant—gold watches, overcoats, houses, waistcoats, and the like.

6. A useful summary of the Gospel of Wealth philosophy in that of Ralph Gabriel, *The Course of American Democratic Thought* (New York, 1939), chapter 13.

7. Harry is inspired by a life of Franklin which he wins as a school prize to travel to the city to make his fortune. His great opportunity raises an interesting ethical point which Alger neatly disregards. Harry is robbed of $40 and his overcoat; the thief, however, leaves his own overcoat behind and Harry finds in it the loot from its owner's previous robberies, totaling $97. This gives Harry a clear profit of $57 which starts him on his way. He never things of notifying the police.

8. See the discussion of this point by John G. Cawelti, "Portrait of the Newsboy as a Young Man," *Wisconsin Magazine of History,* XLV (Winter 1962), 79-83.

9. Fred Schroeder, "America's First Literary Realist," *Western Humanities Review,* XVII (Spring 1963), 129-37; and Robert P. Falk, "Notes on the Higher Criticism of Horatio Alger, Jr.," *Arizona Quarterly,* XIX (Summer 1963), 151-64, deal interestingly with this aspect of Alger's work.

10. Patten's career is chronicled in Harriet Hinsdale and Tony London, eds., *Frank Merriwell's Father: An Autobiography* by Gilbert Patten (Norman, Okla., 1964); and John L. Cutler, "Gilbert Patten and His Frank Merriwell Saga," *University of Maine Studies* (Orono, Me., 1934), series 2, no. 31.

11. Frank once played a game of pool, but only to defeat a pool shark who hoped to victimize one of Frank's friends. As for whiskey—" 'I do not want liquor,' Frank's voice remained on an even keel, 'and I will thank you to put away that flask. Don't you know that you can't drink *that* and play good baseball?' " Dick Merriwell put the case against cigarettes thus: "Cigarettes dull the faculties, stunt and retard the physical development, unsettle the mind, and rob the persistent user of will power and the ability to concentrate."

12. This was spectacularly illustrated by a thug hired to break Frank's arm before the big ball game. Frank fells his attacker and then befriends

him, leading to the thug's immortal line, "I don't know w'y it is, but jes' bein' wid youse makes me want ter do de square t'ing."

13. Patten wrote that he deliberately made Dick Merriwell hot-tempered so that he could force him to learn to discipline himself as an example. See Hinsdale and London, *op. cit.*, 240.

14. Patten himself fought the Klan in New Jersey in the twenties, and in 1939 wrote a radio script for the Council Against Intolerance in which Frank Merriwell defended a Jewish ballplayer at Fardale.

15. A good account of the Stratemeyer syndicate is "For It Was Indeed He," *Fortune*, IX (April 1934), 194 ff. Exactly how many books it produced, and under what names, is not yet fully known. According to some estimates, Stratemeyer wrote 100 volumes himself under various names, 50 under his own, and devised plots for 800 more done by hired writers.

16. Stratemeyer's formula called for exactly 50 jokes per book, no embracing or kissing girls, and either exclamation points or a question at the end of each chapter.

17. However, two of Tom's inventions have not yet been duplicated, his diamond-making machine (which made not industrial diamonds but blue-white gems as large as a golf-ball), and his silencer for airplane motors, which jet-plane manufacturers would dearly love to borrow. Stratemeyer and Garis were extremely clever in their use of pseudo-science, using convincing language and explaining the processes in detail, except for a good deal of fuzziness about essentials. Tom's revolutionary storage battery, for example, which drove his electric runabout at thirty miles an hour, used oxide of nickel, steel, and iron oxide electrodes in a solution of lithium hydrate. It won't work, of course, but it sounded so good that any boy who read the book could converse knowledgeably about nickel oxide and lithium hydrate with his friends until they read it too.

18. In 1954 Grosset and Dunlap initiated a Tom Swift, Jr., series, in which Tom's son invented such things as Tomasite plastic (casings for nuclear reactors), a Swift Spectrograph that analyzed anything in an instant, and a Damonscope (named after gentle, bumbling Mr. Damon) which detected fluorescence, or something, in space.

Folklore

and

Popular

Culture

Catalysts for Interdisciplinary Study

Donald M. Winkelman

This section, devoted to Folklore and Popular Culture, includes a group of papers whose importance goes beyond their obvious merit as scholarly documents. These essays demonstrate the study of folklore materials themselves; they also show folklore as a catalyst for interdisciplinary study which brings together literature, history, anthropology, and musicology, and leads toward the analysis, evaluation, and more complete comprehension of diverse cultural manifestations. The papers do not limit themselves to American culture as it is conceived in the limited European-oriented sense of the word; nor are the subjects concerned with the close analysis of minutiae. Rather, they are bold ventures into not entirely conventional areas which, in time, will be essential for every researcher involved with cultural analysis.

Ray B. Browne's paper on popular theater in *Moby Dick* in a way extends the approach developed by Russel B. Nye on popular culture and sets the stage for Tristram P. Coffin's "Real Use and Real Abuse of Folklore in the Writer's Subconscious." Coffin examines the appearance of folklore in literature and discusses its relationship to the writer. The paper is another step in the formulation of a critical technique based on analysis of tales, anecdotes, beliefs, and ideas in folk tradition which find their way into art-literature.

Both Bruno Nettl and Américo Paredes are concerned with intercultural manifestations. Nettl's "Influences of Western Civilization on North American Indian Music" combines anthropological and musicological approaches to enrich our knowledge of ethnomusicological phenomena and cross-cultural influences. At the same time, he adds another dimension to our knowledge of American Indians and parallels the work of Stith Thompson, who studied enculturated European tales among North American Indians.

Paredes' paper, "The Anglo-American in Mexican Folklore," is another view of "The Ugly American," and may be the type of study which has relevance beyond folklore, sociology, and anthropology. This paper points to the ideas, stereotypes, and images which would enable our foreign service officers to comprehend the thinking of the people in the various areas in which they are stationed and consequently to do a better job of making the American point of view understood. Indeed, Paredes highlights the need for the establishment of cultural commissions which could and should be a part of every ambassadorial staff.

Various approaches to the ballad have been tried since Shakespeare's sprightly comments in the sixteenth century. C. E. Nelson's "Ballard of Thomas Rhymer: Its Eighteenth-century Origin and Its Subsequent Tradition" provides an historical view and the ramifications of a particularly interesting ballad which was last collected in America. Donald M. Winkelman's "Toward a Rhythmic Definition of the Child Ballads" seeks the form and structure of the musical rhythm of the Child ballad. Although ballad poetry has been the subject of a good deal of scholarly analysis, little has been done with the music, and even less with musical rhythm. This paper provides a partial remedy.

The value of these papers is the directions they indicate for future study. The literary, the musical, the historical, and the traditional are combined in a way which demonstrate clearly the unity of cultural manifestations.

Popular Theater in *Moby Dick*

Ray B. Browne

Despite the large body of scholarship on *Moby Dick* by writers interested in the effect of American civilization on Melville,[1] one aspect of this subject has completely escaped attention. There is in this book heavy and light legitimate drama, as everybody knows—Shakespeare's Lear and Fool—but there is also use of the popular theater which constitutes a minor but significant theme that informs both the Shakespearean elements and the other aspects. By "popular theater" I mean the various kinds of theater of the mid-nineteenth century which appealed to the people in general, as distinguished from the "legitimate" theater: burlesques, extravaganzas, farces, variety acts, curtain-raisers, entr'actes, melodramas—and, of course, Negro minstrels. Although both white and black face shows were the same body with different colored faces, Melville generally separated them, especially to emphasize the importance of the blackness of the latter;[2] therefore in this study I usually distinguish between them.

Melville must have known the popular theater well. It was everywhere around him.

As Rourke commented: "Through the 40's and 50's the spirit of burlesque was abroad in the land like a powerful genie let out of a windbag."[3] Melville was indeed interested in the "spirit of burlesque," as Matthiessen said. This is clearly demonstrated in his early, sophomoric exercises in the Albany *Microscope* and his nine "Authentic Anecdotes of 'Old Zack' " which appeared in *Yankee Doodle*. Had Melville not learned about it from the stage itself, he would have got a knowledge of the popular theater from the various songbooks of the day. He was a lover of songs and singing. While on the *Acushnet* he and Toby Greene whiled away "many pleasant moonlight watches" "with yarn and

89

song till 'eight bells',," Toby reminded him after being discovered alive. Melville wrote to Hawthorne, furthermore, at the time that *Moby Dick* was being burningly set to paper that his picture of heaven included "humorous and comic songs."[4] Finally, Melville would have learned about the comic theater from his fellow sailors and whaling men. On whaling ships, for example, the dog-watch was generally spent by the men in singing and dancing. Whaling men carried pocket songsters (small songbooks) with them on their long voyages.[5] In addition to songs, these books contained skits and passages of stage humor. Melville is known to have been interested in such books and to have consulted them.[6]

On the popular stage there was a general lack of seriousness, a broad humor, a knowing wink at the audience, all of which are characteristics of *Moby Dick,* and qualities that Melville obviously enjoyed. Thus Melville found in this stage copy, material which pleased him and which could be utilized in his work.

The influence of the popular theater is not always obvious. Sometimes it is subtle and intricate. But it is never extraneous, because all elements in the book are functional. Further, this influence explains why in *Moby Dick* Melville sounds at times like fantastic Shakespeare, when, as Matthiessen said, he is "lumbering" and his "humor runs thin." Melville knew what he was doing, however much his readers do not.

That *Moby Dick* is theatrically oriented Melville makes clear at the very beginning; that it is framed in drama is made clear in the "Epilogue," which begins, "The drama's done." In the beginning, in "Loomings," Melville sandwiches Ishmael's name on "the bill" between an announcement of an election for the U. S. Presidency and a battle in Afghanistan. Ishmael cannot be sure why he was put "down for this shabby part of a whaling voyage, when others were set down for magnificent parts in high tragedies, and short and easy parts in genteel comedies, and jolly parts in farces." Further, Melville demonstrates that he knows the theater from top to bottom when he says that Ishmael's going a-whaling "came in as a sort of brief interlude and solo between more extensive performances"—which was common practice on the stage of the day —and he implies at least that the voyage will be more popular theater than legitimate.

The second hint of the popular theater motif—that of minstrelsy —comes in the next chapter. Ishmael has just arrived in New Bedford and is wandering around the cold street looking for a cheap lodging. He strays through a door "invitingly open," which had a "careless look, as if it were meant for the uses of the public." He has entered a Negro church, "A great Black Parliament sitting in Tophet." But discovering his mistake, he hastily backs out, muttering to himself and revealing the bent of his mind if not his overt purpose: "No entertainment" in this place, he remarks.

What is likely a popular theater reference is introduced, again, when Ishmael goes into another church, that of Father Mapple, on Sunday. Father Mapple ascends the rope ladder to his prow-pulpit, then deliberately pulls his rope ladder up behind him, thus isolating himself in his "little Quebec." Ishmael, pondering this act for some time, lets his mind wander to the theater—popular or serious—for he cannot believe that the preacher, "who enjoyed such a wide reputation for sincerity and sanctity," could be accused of "courting notoriety by any mere tricks of the stage." That Melville is ironic about the real character of Father Mapple here is irrelevant to the point.

The popular theater motif is definitely established when Ishmael applies to the *Pequod* to sign up for the whaling voyage. Captains Peleg and Bildad are stereotype characters straight from the popular stage. They shout, they use extravagant gestures, their language is overly dramatic. Peleg even threatens standard minstrel violence: "Dost see that leg?" he asks Ishmael, "I'll take that leg away from thy stern, if ever thou talkest of the marchant service to me again." Ishmael expected at least the 275th lay as his earnings for the voyage and would not have been surprised had he been offered the 200th. But when Peleg asks Bildad what lay Ishmael should be given Bildad answers with the face of the popular theater straight man: "Thou knowest best," was the sepul-chral[7] reply, "the seven hundred and seventy-seventh wouldn't be too much, would it?" The two captains even engage in stagy horse-play: "Out of this cabin, ye canting, drab-colored son of a wooden gun—a straight wake with ye!" shouts Peleg. "As he thundered out this he made a rush at Bildad, but with a marvellous oblique, sliding celerity, Bildad for that time eluded him."

This atmosphere is further maintained when Queequeg is brought aboard to sign up. Bildad, impressed with the promising harpooner, wants to engage him. Though nobody else has had difficulty understanding and pronouncing his name, Peleg, with a touch of the popular theater, mauls it almost beyond recognition: He says: "We must have Hedgehog there, I mean Quohog, in one of our boats."

In *Moby Dick* events usually come in doublets, one backing and commenting on the other. So chapter 29 ("Enter Ahab; to him, Stubb"), in which Ahab tells Stubb, "Down dog, and kennel," which is an echo of *Lear*, is backed by chapter 31 ("Queen Mab"). In it, Stubb recounts a strange dream he had after being insulted by Ahab. In this dream he was kicking away at a pyramid, when

> a sort of badger-haired old merman, with a hump on his back, takes me by the shoulders, and slews me round. "What are you 'bout?" says he. Slid! man, but I was frightened. Such a phiz! but, somehow next moment I was over the fright. "What am I about?" says I at last. "And what business is that of yours, I should like to know, Mr. Humpback? Do *you* want a kick?" [Stubb's reference, and his slang, reintroduces Peleg's threat to kick Ishmael and the popular theater motif, which is carried on in Stubb's further report.] "By the lord, Flask, I had no sooner said that, than he turned round his stern to me, bent over, and dragging up a lot of seaweed he had for a clout—what do you think I saw?—why thunder alive, man, his stern was stuck full of marlinspikes, with the points out."

The parallel here with *Romeo and Juliet* is obvious. But these sailor-version *anus dentatus* are not from the legitimate stage presentation. Rather the parallel must be to the tradition of the popular theater adaptation. Shakespeare was the most popular single author in American popular theater. There were hundreds of books of songs and jokes, gags and conundrums, burlesques and travesties in which he was used in every conceivable way. *Romeo and Juliet* was one of the most widespread.[8] An example, from a somewhat later period, will illustrate.

Entitled *Roamy-E-Owe and Julie-Ate,* it begins after the party, at which Benvolio, Mercutio and Roamy-E-Owe stuffed themselves. Tybalt upbraids the trio for coming to the supper uninvited, then he tweaks Roamy-E-Owe's nose, hits his jaw and kicks him. Roamy-E-Owe then does the same to Tybalt, who snivels and goes away. Julie-Ate tells R: "Roamy-O-Owe, Roamy-O-Owe, wherefore are thou Roamy-O-Owe? A strong onion would smell as sweet called by any other name. What's in a name? The [local river or some ill-smelling point] is just as sweet, no matter what you call it." J. asks R. if he has a dime, for she wants a bucket of beer, since she has had only "six steins tonight" and her "tongue is parched." The two plan to escape in R's automobile, or if they are frustrated, they will drink poison. J. wants hers with a cherry in it. R. buys some "German stuff" from a doctor-apothecary, whose patients always die. At the time of their elopement, they are caught and a dog digs into R's pants as he climbs over a wall. No one dies.

The closest known parallel to Melville, which also was too extreme for presentation—at least to a mixed audience—is the somewhat later burlesque "The Royal Nonesuch" in *Huckleberry Finn,* in which the King cavorts around the stage naked, "painted all over, ring-streaked-and-striped, all sorts of colors as splendid as a rainbow."

In *Moby Dick,* after a lapse of two chapters, the popular theater material is reintroduced in "The Cabin-Table" (chapter 34), which burlesques propriety in its account of the order of precedence in which Ahab and the mates descend to the table to eat. When Flask, "the third Emir," is alone on deck before being called down, "tipping all sorts of knowing winks in all sorts of directions, and kicking off his shoes, he strikes into a sharp but noiseless squall of a hornpipe right over the Grand Turk's head," then brings "up the rear with music," but "ships a new face" before stepping into the presence of Ahab, "in the character of Abjectus, or the Slave."

Next, use of the popular stage continues in one of Melville's most effective and intensely dramatic scenes, chapter 36, "The Quarter-Deck." Ahab has gathered the men around him and nailed the golden doubloon to the mainmast. He has forced the men madly to pledge allegiance to him and to the destruction of the white whale. The three mates have been stared down. Starbuck, the first mate, stands alone on the stage, soliloquizing: "My soul is more than matched; she's overmanned; and by a madman!" As he thinks further, his reveries are interrupted by "A burst of revelry from the forecastle," as the stage direction gives it. "Oh, God!" meditates Starbuck, "that revelry is forward! mark the unfaltering silence aft." Then, in chapter 37, as dusk approaches, Melville switches to Stubb, the thoughtless, jolly mate, who will go to his destruction, as he says, "laughing." Stubb sings a song which is a stage direction pointing to the next chapter:

We'll drink tonight, with hearts as light,
  To love, as gay and fleeting
As bubbles that swim, on the beaker's brim,
  And break on the lips while meeting.

The next chapter (38) is "Midnight, Forecastle." The revelry which so shatteringly interrupted and commented on Starbuck's reverie earlier in the day now has peaked. Whalemen are singing and talking about girls. They want "a jig or two." For their musician they call upon Pip. Pip is a nonprofessional musician, an amateur Negro minstrel. Melville says of him: "In his native Tolland County in Connecticut, he had once enlivened many a fiddler's frolic on the green; and at melodious even-tide, with his gay ha-ha! had turned the round horizon into one star-belled tambourine," mentioning the one musical instrument particularly symbolic of minstrelsy. Melville's further description of Pip is trite and so directly contradictory to Melville's real feeling about the Negro that it can only be interpreted as pointing up Pip's "staginess:" "With that pleasant, genial, jolly brightness peculiar to his tribe, a tribe, which ever enjoy all holidays and festivities with finer, freer relish than any other race."

Pip reluctantly agrees to play his tambourine. But the activity is interrupted by lightning and a squall. All hands tumble up to save the ship, leaving Pip alone to comment on the scene and predict the future. The thought of the white whale makes him "jingle all over like [his] tambourine." Thus here the minstrel motif is left in suspension to be picked up and intensified later.

The minstrel motif is carried on in the powerfully dramatic chapter 64, "Stubb's Supper", in which Stubb, having killed his whale, demands a whale steak. It has been said that the Cook's sermon is "comic in the frontier fashion."[9] But in fact both the cook and the sermon are more from Negro minstrelsy. "This old Fleece, as they called him, came shuffling and limping along, assisting his step with his tongs, which, after a clumsy fashion, were made of straightened iron hoops." Fleece's exhortation is a minstrel mock sermon, the dialect that of the Negro stage: "Your woraciousness, fellow-critturs, I don't blame ye so much for; dat is natur, and can't be helped; but to gobern dat wicked natur, dat is de pint."

More popular theater is introduced in the meeting of the *Pequod* and the *Rose-Bud,* when Stubb conspires with the Guernsey chief-mate of the latter to relieve the French ship of the blasted whale which is tied alongside. In a veritable comedy of diddling, the chief-mate mistranslates everything that Stubb says to the Frenchman, in a scene which can only be looked upon as burlesque. It is popular theater at its best—or worst.

Humor that was of the burlesque stage, or just one step away from it, is introduced in the next chapter, "Ambergris" (92). Melville is in a sportive mood about the paradox of this sweet substance coming from the bowels of the whale. Earlier, he had found humor about the bowels irresistible. In chapter 81, "The

Pequod Meets the Virgin," for example, Stubb is chasing a "huge, humped old bull," the spout of which was "short, slow, and laborious; coming forth with a choking sort of gush, and spending itself in torn shreds, followed by strange subterranean commotions in him, which seemed to have egress at his other buried extremity, causing the waters behind him to upbubble." Stubb cannot resist referring to what must have been a whalers' joke: "Who's got some paregoric? He has the stomach ache. Adverse winds are holding mad Christmas in him, boys. It's the first foul wind I ever knew to blow from astern."

Melville's delight in the subject continues into the chapter on "Ambergris," in which he says that one cause for the creation of the substance is supposed to be dyspepsia. "How to cure such a dyspepsia it were hard to say, unless by administering three or four boat loads of Brandreth's pills, and then running out of harm's way, as laborers do in blasting rocks."

From this joke, which must have been widespread among sailors, Melville turns to another which must have been even more common. Among whalers unnatural sexual relations were endemic, and jokes about copulation between man and whale! Melville says: "I have forgotten to say that there were found in this ambergris, certain hard, round, bony plates, which at first Stubb thought might be sailors' trousers buttons." Such a joke would have been merely the salt-water version of the type of humor ubiquitous on land, circulated for example in the numerous Crockett almanacs, which Melville had written for. In the Crockett *Awl-Man-Axe* for 1839, for instance, there is the joke about "The Height of Folly," which is "being so tall that you are obliged to climb a ladder to shave yourself."[10] This type of joke is still a favorite genre of folk humor today. A widespread example is: "Do you know what the height of folly is? A flea crawling up an elephant's leg with rape on his mind."

That Melville was not above such humor is evidenced by his references in other books, and to his use of it in the climactic third day of the chase of Moby Dick. As the *Pequod* sinks beneath the waves, Stubb, resigned to death, still thinks of life, and says, "For me, off shoes and jacket to it; let Stubb die in his drawers! . . . cherries! cherries! cherries! Oh, Flask, for one red cherry ere we die!' " And Flask, misunderstanding the sexual implications, merely replies: " 'Cherries! I only wish that we were where they grow'."[11] Further, the whole chapter 95, "The Cassock" is built on what must have been rough sailor humor, on "the grandissimus, as the mariners call it," which is "longer than a Kentuckian is tall." The whale's penis is skinned and provides a protective hood for the man boiling the try-works. In another obvious play on the grotesque in sexual implications he puns on two levels: the *Jung-frau*, the German ship which is inferior to the American as a whaler, is without whale oil and has to borrow from the American. Thus this ship is a virgin because innocent of lamp sperm, the source of light and life, but on a lower lever virginally innocent of whale sperm! Much earlier, in the chapter entitled "Stubb's Supper," Stubb in speaking to the cook orders a diet which must be understood on two levels: "Whaleballs for breakfast—don't forget," which on one level must, in referring to "Mountain oysters, of gigantic proportions" have made one of the most gargantuan and repulsive breakfasts in frontier exaggeration.

Chapter 93, "The Castaway," focuses on Pip, and Melville reminds us of the Negro's minstrel aspect: "Poor Pip! ye have heard of him before; ye must remember his tambourine on that dramatic midnight, so gloomy-jolly."

Pip's idiocy, which resulted from being abandoned in the sea by Stubb, is picked up and developed only five chapters later, in the magnificent chapter 99, "The Doubloon." This chapter is the quintessence of the whole book. It is the first climax, the projection of the conclusion. It too is built on humor of the popular stage, the kind that Rosenberry called "dramatic-structural:" "The artist . . . deploys his comic forces to expose the vital interplay of character and situation and performs the successful act of creation that fuses the disparate elements of comedy and tragedy into a balanced work of art."

The doubloon pictures the remarkable *roundness* of the whole book. The book is beautifully *centered,* the center of ambiguity between extremes. But the roundness symbolizes more, as many references indicate. In *Moby Dick* the center is God, "the centre and circumference of all democracy" (chapter 26); it is the "tremendous centralization" of "an imperial brain," before which "the plebeian herds crouch abased," and about which "the tragic dramatist who would depict mortal indomitableness in its fullest sweet and direct swing," cannot forget a hint, incidentally so important in his art" (chapter 33); it is Ahab, whose "dogged circle" fits into his men's "various wheels, and they revolve" (chapter 38); it is "great hearts" which "sometimes condense to one deep pang, the sum total of those shallow pains kindly diffused through feebler men's whole lives . . . for even in their pointless centres, these noble natures contain the entire circumferences of inferior souls" (chapter 133).

By slight extension the circle is the viscera, the bowels, the umbilicus, procreation and death and resurrection which, again, numerous quotes illustrate. In chapter 87, "The Grand Armada," the whalemen were "in that enchanged calm which they say lurks at the heart of every commotion. And still in the distracted distance we beheld the tumults of the outer concentric circles, and and saw successive pods of whales, eight or ten in each, swiftly going round and round, like multiplied spans of horses in a ring." In this stillness Queequeg and Starbuck see "long coils of the umbilical cord of Madame Leviathan, by which the young cub seemed still tethered to its dam." Further, "some of the subtlest secrets of the seas seemed divulged to us in this enchanted pond. We saw young Leviathan amours in the deep." When squeezing out the sperm in "A Squeeze of the Hand," (chapter 94), fingers begin "to serpentine and spiralize." In the chapter called "The Fossil Whale" (104), Melville says: "Since I have undertaken to manhandle this Leviathan, it behoves me to approve myself omnisciently exhaustive in the enterprise; not overlooking the minutest seminal germs of his blood, and spinning him out to the uttermost coil of his bowels." Finally, as the *Pequod,* battered by Moby Dick, sinks beneath the waves, "concentric circles seized the lone boat itself, and all its crew, and each floating oar, and every lancepole, and spinning, animate and inanimate, all round and round in one vortex, carried the smallest chip of the *Pequod* out of sight" (chapter 135).

But it must be remembered that out of this circle Ishmael was resurrected: "Round and round, then, and ever contracting towards the button-like black bubble at the apex of that slowly wheeling circle, like another Ixion I did revolve. Till, gaining that vital centre, the black bubble upward burst; and now . . . rising with great force, the coffin life-buoy shot lengthwise from the sea, fell over, and floated by my side" (Epilogue).

The significance of the doubloon chapter is thus manifest. The setting is of the stage. Stubb stands by, hidden, while various members of the crew come by to soliloquize. Each person shapes the symbology into his own likeness. The last to speak is Pip: " 'Here's the ship's navel, this doubloon here, and they are all on fire to unscrew it. But, unscrew your navel, and what's the consequence? . . . Cook! ho, cook! and cook us! Jenny! hey, hey, hey, hey, hey, Jenny, Jenny! and get your hoe-cake done!' "

Vincent and Mansfield have remarked on the "omphalos symbolism" of the reference to the navel as being the center of life and being. But there is more. Melville had said in chapter 49, "There are certain queer times and occasions in this strange mixed affair we call life when a man takes this whole universe for a vast practical joke, though the wit thereof he but dimly discerns, and more than suspects that the joke is at nobody's expense but his own." Melville here is carrying this serious joke forward. For he is working in the common popular theater joke of the day that if you unscrew your navel your rear end will fall off.[12]

Pip ends his speech with a shuffle, while singing "Jenny, get your hoe-cake done," a minstrel song immensely popular at the time, as Willard Thorpe has recognized.[13] This practice of having patter ended with a shuffle was, of course, the very fiber of minstrelsy. An illustration with a bit of minstrel Shakespeare, ending with the most famous of the "jump" songs will be informative:

> Oh! 'tis consummation
> Devoutly to be wished,
> To end your heartache by a sleep;
> When likely to be dished,
> Shuffle off your mortal coil,
> Do just so,
> Wheel about and turn about
> And jump Jim Crow.[14]

Now with the minstrel aspect firmly established, Melville carries on the popular theater motif while having the *Pequod* meet, in the next chapter, the *Samuel Enderby*, of London. This is a zany ship, straight from a nineteenth-century *Hellzapoppin*. The Captain has lost his arm to Moby Dick, and wears an ivory one. Ahab is brought to the deck of the *Enderby* by sitting on a blubber-hook, surely as undignified an entry as he could have had. As soon as Ahab touches the deck, the other captain approaches: "and Ahab, putting out his ivory leg, and crossing the ivory arm (like two sword-fish blades) cried out in his walrus way, 'Aye, aye, hearty! let us shake bones together.'" Never before has Ahab had a "walrus" voice, and never has he been so hearty. The zany captain is companioned with other fantastics. His name is Boomer, his surgeon's name is Bunger, his first mate's name is Mounttop, and the others, who are unnamed, probably have similar appellations. Rosenberry recognized that these people are straight from the stage. Indeed they are. And the significance of the confrontation between these men and Ahab is portentous. They are lighthearted. Boomer is not sorry he lost his arm to

Moby Dick; he is delighted that he lost no more. But Ahab is dark and terrifying. Here on the same stage popular theater faces tragedy, and tragedy stalks away to its ruin. Boomer's arm remains intact. But Ahab quits the *Samuel Enderby* so precipitately that he half splinters his leg and has it replaced.

Back on the *Pequod,* Ahab sends for the carpenter to build a new leg. Here Melville reverses his usual order of having light comedy follow serious drama; instead he has the carpenter, standing before his vice-bench trying to be serious while making a man, burlesqueing his own seriousness by sneezing in the middle of every stroke of work and every half thought. His feelings are callous and indifferent, but he turns to lighthearted banter: " 'If I but only had the time, I could turn him [Ahab] out as neat a leg now as ever (*sneezes*) scraped to a lady in a parlor.' " This is obviously Shakespeare, but more Shakespeare spoofed than straight.

We next see mad Pip when he wanders in to talk to Queequeg, who, as all believe, is sick unto death and is testing the comfort of his newly built coffin. Pip draws near, and "holding his tambourine" says: " 'Poor rover! Will ye never have done with all this weary roving?' " The words are probably a paraphrase of those of the chorus of a widely sung sea-song generally called "A-Roving:"

A-roving, a-roving
Since roving's been my ruin
I'll go no more a-roving
With you, fair maid.[15]

Then Pip shakes his tambourine and says: " 'Rig-a-dig, dig dig! Now, Queequeg, die; and I'll beat ye your dying march'."

Starbuck replies to Pip, and in this speech Melville carries on the theater motif by echoing *Julius Caesar* (II, ii): " 'I have heard that in violent fevers, men, all ignorance, have talked in ancient tongues.' " After another dozen lines Starbuck listens to Pip again. Pip "wildly" picks up the *Caesar* and develops it further: "Form two and two! Let's make a General of him! Ho, where's his harpoon? Lay it across here.—Rig-a-dig, dig dig! huzza! Oh for a game cock now to sit upon his head and crow. Queequeg dies game! mind ye that; Queequeg dies game!"

Melville in developing his burlesque interweaves several aspects. Earlier he had said that Stubb "would hum over his old rigadig tunes while flank and flank with the most exasperated monster." Here Pip quotes these words to contrast his own cowardice with Queequeg's bravery. Queequeg's bravery is, of course, Caesar's:

"Cowards die many times before their deaths: The valiant never taste of death but once." This passage in *Julius Caesar* contains words which, further, make a microcosm of the whole of *Moby Dick*: "What can be avoided whose end is purpos'd by the mighty gods?"

Perhaps the neatest mixture in this passage is Melville's play on the Roman custom of reading the entrails of birds and beasts as auguries, and the popular theater—and general—tradition of the "Game Cock of the Wilderness," a usage which could hardly have escaped the attention of contemporary readers.

When we see Pip again in chapter 125, Melville is reintroducing the joke about the navel. Now, just before the three-day battle with Moby Dick begins, Ahab is battling the elements. He orders the Manxman to heave the log, but the Manxman fears that the line will part. When he does throw it, the line does part, and Ahab says: "I crush the quadrant, the thunder turns the needle, and now the mad sea parts the log-line." As he stalks away, the Manxman remarks: "Where he goes now; to him nothing's happened; but to me, *the skewer seems loosening out of the middle of the world!* (my emphasis)." At this point Pip appears, riveting together the significance of the earlier joke and the fate of the ship.

The magnificent Epilogue blends all elements. The joke about the navel, which by now has become a motif, is given a final comment. Melville returns to his circle-center theme. Ishmael swirls toward the *"button-like black bubble at the axis* of that slowly wheeling circle (my emphasis)," until from it springs his salvation, his resurrection, the coffin on which he rides to safety. In other words, he is resurrected from the belly button of the world.

Moby Dick is a many-stranded rope, intricately wound. Melville's use of material from the popular theater strengthens the fiber of the book as a whole. No other American—not even Hawthorne —has taken material intrinsically so slight and woven it so thematically and profoundly into a work of art.

Notes

1. See especially Daniel G. Hoffman, *Form and Fable in American Fiction* (New York, 1961); Richard Chase, *Herman Melville* (New York, 1949); F. O. Matthiessen, *American Renaissance* (New York, 1941).

Richard Chase in *Herman Melville* (New York, 1949, 102) remarks that Melville was not called upon to "invent the central epic theme" of *Moby Dick;* "that was given to him by his culture; he had merely to recognize it." He needed only to "adduce the body of supporting mythology, clothe the skeleton with flesh and the habiliments of style. For this purpose 'all things' were grist for the mill—jokes, puns, dances, ceremonies, side shows, catalogues, scientific discourses, orations, meditations, confessions, sermons, tall tales, redactions of Old World mythologies, and literary conventions."

2. On this subject in general, see Harry Levin, *The Power of Blackness* (New York, 1958).

3. Constance Rourke, *American Humor* (New York, 1931), 155.

4. Jay Leyda, *The Melville Log* (New York, 1951), II, 632, 413.

5. See one of the books that Melville drew on heavily for *Moby Dick,* J. Ross Browne, *Etchings of a Whaling Cruise* (New York, 1846) 111. For the degree to which Melville used this book, see Howard P. Vincent, *The Trying-Out of Moby Dick* (Cambridge, Mass., 1949).

6. Merton M. Sealts, Jr., "Melville's Reading," *Harvard Library Bulletin,* II, No. 3 (Autumn 1948), items 407, 411.

7. A "sepulchral" voice was one of the most well-worn techniques of the popular stage. See, for example, "De Darkey Tragedian," *The Ethiopian Drama,* No. 92 (New York, 1874). On the general subject, see Carl Wittke, *Tambo and Bones* (Durham, N. C., 1930).

8. See R. B. Browne, "Shakespeare in American Vaudeville and Negro Minstrelsy," *American Quarterly,* XII (Fall 1960), 374-91.

9. Hoffman, *Form and Fable,* 269.

10. Chase, *Melville,* 72.

11. For a different interpretation of the cherry references, see Alan Heimert, "Moby Dick and American Political Symbolism," *American Quarterly,* XV (Winter 1963), 498-534. Heimert would apparently connect this reference to George Washington.

12. John D. Seelye, "The Golden Navel: The Cabalism of Ahab's Doubloon," *Nineteenth Century Fiction,* XIV (March 1960), 350-55.

13. Willard Thorp, ed., *Moby Dick, or the Whale* (New York, 1947), 408.

14. "Shakespeare in American Vaudeville and Negro Minstrelsy," 382.

15. William M. Doerflinger, *Shantymen and Shantyboys* (New York, 1951), 51. Melville's lines are close, too, it should be noticed, to Byron's "So We'll Go No More A-Roving," and Byron was well known to Melville.

Real Use and Real Abuse
of Folklore in The Writer's Subconscious:
F. Scott Fitzgerald

Tristram P. Coffin

The asininity and arrogance of the psychologists and mythographers who have undertaken literary interpretation in the last few decades rages on. I used to think that Erich Fromm's idiotic interpretation of "Little Red Cap" (his loaded name for "Little Red Riding Hood")[1] was a nadir below which this school could not sink, but I was naive. Since that essay, in 1951, a blaze of equally preposterous remarks on everything from *Hamlet* to *The Hamlet* has consumed scholarship. The latest I recall is a dilly—the theory being that Tom Sawyer, when he enters the cave in Twain's novel, is working out his Oedipus complex by means of a symbolic intercourse with Mother Earth.

I just don't understand scholars who think this way. They are well-trained people, coming from the best graduate schools, teaching at the best universities. Generally they hold a deep scorn for inadequate research and sloppy logic. They hate ignorance. But somehow they can't see how they are guilty of these faults themselves. They are quite insensitive to the fact that depth analyses of various cultures have negated many of the superficial similarities fascinating to the comparative mythologists of earlier generations. They fail to recognize that the interpretation of symbolic language in multiple variants of a myth usually creates paradoxes. They don't seem to know that something like Sophocles' *Oedipus Rex* is a literary reworking of mythological and legendary matter and therefore cannot be treated as folk. They don't recognize that while America has developed a national subliterary lore, its folklore has remained regional, occupational, and ethnic in focus. They seem to have no idea of how old märchen actually are, how long history can survive in oral tradition, or exactly how ritual does persist. They are psychologists, interpreting written and oral literatures about which they know little. They are literary critics, interpreting psychological and anthropological evidence about which they know little. They are scholars who use terms like "archetype," "myth," "reality," "American folk," "fable," and "legend" so loosely and so casually they have made the words almost meaningless.

In my really cynical moments, I explain their behavior this way: (1) each generation of scholars has to have a gimmick so it can rewrite all the articles of the past, build a bibliography of "fresh" interpretations, and deserve its promotions and grants; (2) irrational symbolic language offers an area in which one cannot be proved wrong and in which one can always defend himself by patronizing the attacker; (3) the political atmosphere in the world today encourages the "discovery" of archetypes and other indications that all men are one and the same. And I suppose most people can't resist the opportunity of new frontiers, *cartes blanches,* immunity from error, and the chance to prove Sophocles, the Watusi, and Oscar Wilde brothers under the skin.

When I am cynical, I am probably right, for cynics usually are. But being right is not my present concern. What really bothers me here is the fact that these scholars have made it all but impossible to talk sensibly about the subconscious use of folklore by a literary genius. One either talks in the sweeping generalities of Frazer, Rank, and Raglan or he talks not at all.

I recall trying to publish the article that has been revised to make up the bulk of this paper. It finally appeared in *Midwest Folklore* under the title "Gatsby's Fairy Lover"[2] after it had been rejected by a very prominent journal. The rejection embittered me, not because the article was deemed unworthy, but because of the reader's sole comment—erased, though still legible, on the cover: "I wouldn't accept this; we have published enough of that myth-ritual stuff already." Now I know who the reader was (his name was also not properly erased) and I know he is a prominent Fitzgerald scholar. Assuming he read the article (and I am certain he did), I can only explain his remark as an instance of preconditioning in the sort of scholarship I have been debunking. Evidently the reader could not believe an article about the subconscious use of folklore in *The Great Gatsby* could be anything except another example of what he erroneously labeled "myth-ritualism." That a scholar this prominent can be this confused is really tragic.

For obviously a writer may use folklore, or any other material for that matter, subconsciously, and be doing nothing more than just that. He may simply call on formulas and motifs gathered from his reading and observations, developing them without an awareness that he has used then—and he may do this without mythic association, without psychic symbolism, without sharing his usage with other minds in his or another culture. The fact that the formulas and motifs have complicated histories or even that they can be traced to myth or ritual is often irrelevant. In fact, it is likely that most uses to which writers put folk materials offer thin pickings in a cross-cultural sense and really prove little except a man must write out of those things he has put into his own mind—"experience, the universal Mother of Science," being also the universal Mother of Art.[3]

Fitzgerald was such a writer. He used folklore and matter derived from folklore steadily, always to be sure generalizing it and refocusing it, but nonetheless using it so integrally one needs to know the folk backgrounds to get a full understanding of the works. Broad themes from Celtic fairy lore and the märchen lie behind many of his tales and novels: "the land of no time," "the vanishing lover," "the golden girl in the white palace," "the underdog hero," "the magic power of money," "the reality of happiness-ever-after." Such motifs, tied up more intimately with his private life than with his American culture background, need no symbolic interpretation, disguise no mythic patterns. Certainly, they are unique for Fitzgerald as he develops them. They distinguish him from, rather than bind him to, other peoples, other Irish-Americans, other graduates of Princeton, just as they are meaningless in the works of his contemporaries Hemingway, Eliot, Frost, or Budd Schulberg.

A penetrating discussion by Richard L. Schoenwald entitled "F. Scott Fitzgerald as John Keats"[4] clearly establishes Fitzgerald's debt to the Englishman in matters all the way from vocabulary to overall inspiration. Schoenwald's remarks concentrate heavily on *Tender is the Night,* and he discusses *The Great Gatsby* only in passing. He might well have spent more time on Fitzgerald's masterpiece, for *The Great Gatsby* uses the basic situation of Keats's *La Belle Dame Sans Merci* as its foundation.[5]

Keats's *La Belle Dame Sans Merci* is an idealistic development of the old ballad of Thomas Rymer, itself a retelling of one of the adventures of Thomas of Erceldoune.[6] The tale that lies behind the folksong, and ultimately behind Keats's poem, is that of the Fairy Queen who seduces a mortal away from earth. Although Keats changes the temper of the narrative from country to court and although he idealizes the whole affair—emphasizing the irresistible charm of the woman, the passion of the love, and the loneliness of the lover—he retains the essential relationship of the tale, that of the normal man who longs for the unattainable girl.

The parallel to Gatsby and Daisy Buchanan is immediately obvious. We are introduced to Gatsby as he stands "alone and palely loitering." Through flashbacks we learn the story of the poor boy and his "faery's child," how she lured him, told him she loved him true, and left him. In fact, so closely does the outline of the novel follow the outline of the poem, it is amazing no one noticed the parallel before.

The Celtic Fairy Queen, of whom Keats makes use, is truly a "full beautiful creature." Her dress is grass-green or white; she rides a belled horse, usually white; she has flowing hair, scented, and sometimes decorated with apple-blossoms. It is no wonder Thomas of Erceldoune once mistook her for the Queen of Heaven. Keats sums up her beauty with the phrase "her hair was long, her foot was light, and her eyes were wild." When we allow for the change in setting, we are struck with how fairy-like Daisy seems too. Though the symbol for her presence is a green light,[7] she dresses in white. When we first meet her with Jordan Baker, the two girls are presented through the sensitive eyes of Nick Carraway as being capable of suspension and even flight, until the earthy Tom Buchanan drops then symbolically to the floor.

> The only completely stationary object in the room was an enormous couch on which two young women were buoyed up as though upon an anchored balloon. They were both in white, and their dresses were rippling and fluttering as if they had just been blown back in after a short flight around the house. I must have stood for a few moments listening to the whip and snap of the curtains and the groan of a picture on the wall. Then there was a boom as Tom Buchanan shut the rear windows and the caught wind died about the room, and the curtains and the rugs and the two young women ballooned slowly to the floor.[8]

Daisy, whose maiden name is Fay (an older word for fairy)[9] continues to be associated with white throughout the book. Jordan Baker recalls her in Louisville "dressed in white" and driving a "little white roadster" (75). She wears white on the day of the accident (115).

White is, to be sure, the color of purity, of the Virgin, and of the bride-to-be. As Fitzgerald uses it, it has a good deal of irony associated with it. It is not without irony as one color of the Celtic Fairy Queen either. The Celtic Fairy is a creature with Satanic connections; some legends even described such beings as the angels who fell in the Revolt from Awe. Daisy, too, has her Satanic side. At least within the framework of her society she is considered fast. Jordan remembers that "wild rumors were circulating about her" (76) and Gatsby was excited by the fact "that many men had already loved" her (148). Yet her reputation only serves to increase her charm in an echoing and nostalgic way.

Her voice is particularly haunting. Keats describes the "belle dame" as making "sweet moan" and singing "a faery's song." Fitzgerald develops a similar idea.

> It was the kind of voice that the ear follows up and down, as if each speech is an arrangement of notes that will never be played again. Her face was sad and lovely with bright things in it, bright eyes and a bright passionate mouth, but there was an excitement in her voice that men who had cared for her found difficult to forget; a singing compulsion, a whispered "Listen," a promise that she had done gay, exciting things just a while since and that there were gay exciting things hovering in the next hour [9-10].

Carraway thinks of the voice as "indiscreet," though that isn't really the word he wants. Gatsby is the one who pin-points it.

> "She's got an indiscreet voice," I remarked. "It's full of —" I hesitated.
> "Her voice is full of money," he said suddenly.
> That was it. I'd never understood it before. It was full of money —that was the inexhaustible charm that rose and fell in it, the jingle of it, the cymbals' song of it—High in a white palace the king's daughter, the golden girl. . . . [120]

Daisy shares the indiscretion and magic that Gatsby and others (including Fitzgerald himself) have long associated with wealth. She does what she wants, she is without care, and she promises what money can bring. Gatsby's love for her is a mixture of desire for a woman and fascination for moving beyond himself.

Socially, Daisy is beyond Gatsby, who even in his youth carried out programs of self-betterment, as far beyond him as any fairy is beyond any mortal. With his "romantic readiness" (2) he turns her into a dream—"the latest dream he ever did dream"— but it is of no more avail than the knight's dream of his fairy love. Out of "the foul dust" of modern America that floats in the wake of such hopes, Fitzgerald develops the tragedy of the book. Gatsby is left where the sedge has withered—frustrated, alone—having "paid a high price for living too long with a single dream" (162).

> He talked a lot about the past, and I gathered that he wanted to recover something, some idea of himself perhaps, that had gone into loving Daisy. His life had been confused and disordered since then, but if he could once return to a certain starting place and go over it all slowly, he could find out what that thing was. . . . (115)
>
> He stretched out his hand desperately as if to snatch only a wisp of air, to save a fragment of the spot that she had made lovely for him. But it was all going by too fast now for his blurred eyes and he knew that he had lost that part of it, the freshest and the best, forever [153].

The knight's frustration rises, of course, from the fact he is mortal and the fairy is not. The frustration of Gatsby is not dissimilar, though things may seem in reverse at first glance. Gatsby is frustrated not because he is mortal, but because the real Daisy is not supernatural—because she cannot unlive five years, because she reacts practically to the death of Myrtle Wilson. However, this real Daisy is but remotely connected with the Daisy that Gatsby loves. He belives in a supernatural girl who can unlive the past, who is capable of the same "intensity" that he is capable of.

> Almost five years! There must have been moments even that afternoon when Daisy tumbled short of his dreams—not through her own fault, but because of the colossal vitality of his illusion. It had gone beyond her, beyond everything. He had thrown himself into it with a creative passion, adding to it all the time, decking it out with every bright feather that drifted his way [97].

It is this creation of Gatsby's hope that deceives him and goes from him, beyond, as it were, the mists of actuality. The real Daisy, a person playing a tired, pointless game, is a member of a "secret society" (18) of the born rich. As Gatsby is not of the group, she looks at him "as she did love" and "makes sweet moan." But she renounces him during the War for a member of her own group, and she does it again over a "plate of cold fried chicken . . . and two bottles of ale" (146) —sans merci.

Fitzgerald describes the development of Gatsby's "romantic readiness" in the short story *Absolution,* which was "intended to be a picture of" Gatsby's early life.[10] Here the young boy learns that there is a glittering world where he can exist free from God's moral truths responsible only to the promptings of his own imagination. Jay Gatsby, once James Gatz, entered such a world, for when he gave up his dream of mounting "to a secret place above the trees" and wed "his unutterable visions" to a girl's "perishable breath," he recreated his life as a fairy tale with Daisy as the heroine.

Now no scholar would be bold enough to claim that Fitzgerald consciously conceived of Gatsby's dream in terms of a formal märchen, but that he thought of Gatsby's dream as a sort of fairy-tale version of life is obvious. Carraway's flash of understanding comes when he realizes Gatsby thinks of Daisy as the king's daughter, the golden girl living high in a white palace (120). Moreover, if we reconstruct what Gatsby expects the story of his affair with Daisy to be, and set it up as a märchen, it would go like this:

1. "High in a white palace" the hero meets "the king's daughter, the golden girl."

2. He possesses a magic with which to win this princess—the fact that he is different from the others she has known, that he seems to know a lot because he knows different things from her (150). "One still October night" he takes the girl because he has no real right to touch her hand. To his lower middle-class midwestern mind, he has married her because she is a "nice" girl (149). She will be his forever and a day as soon as he builds her a castle such as princesses inhabit. She will wait.

3. The third person possesses the wife before the hero can build her the needed castle. This man is an ogre, and the princess longs to be free of him.

4. Five years elapse. The hero has obtained a new magic object, money. He is now able to build the castle. He goes to where she has been taken in order to rescue her. His original magic, his difference from her usual acquaintances, and the old love work again. The ogre attempts to destroy this magic, but he fails. Love is too strong; the hero and the heroine live happily ever after—having completely forgotten the events of the intervening years.

Oddly, this märchen proves to be a variant of a widespread tale commonly known as its Aladdin version.[11] Like all märchen, it has no rigid form. However, the general pattern typed by Aarne and Thompson as #561 is strikingly similar to the fairy-tale Gatsby creates to replace reality.

1. The hero finds a magic object which will perform all the wishes of the owner.

2. By means of the object he builds a magic castle and marries the king's daughter.

3. The magic object is stolen by a third person who wants to possess the wife. The castle and the wife are transported to a distant island.

4. The hero recovers the object with the help of a second magic object which transports the hero to the island. The castle and the princess are restored.

Gatsby's variant contains all the major motifs of A-T 561. The order is somewhat different, but that is not unusual among märchen. The only new element added is the ability of the hero and the heroine to eradicate the five unhappy years. Some readers may feel that Gatsby's "difference" is not a magic power, but a careful reading of the novel does show this to be the charm through which he originally wins Daisy and that it still attracts her five years later. There is also the point that Tom does not actually steal this magic when he first "possesses the wife," but he certainly destroys it in the hotel in New York just before the accident (125-35).

Fitzgerald is no fool. *The Great Gatsby* tells, in a way, the story of the author's own dreams about Ginevra King and Zelda Sayre. That Fitzgerald wished his own life to be a märchen, with Zelda as the princess and money as the magic object, in no way prevented his seeing that a love affair similar to his own could not work as fairy tales might and that money has its limits as far as magic goes. In the novel he sees to it that Gatsby's märchen ends wrong. Daisy's little girl by Tom makes it clear that five years cannot be erased; unhappy fate in the form of the auto accident crushes the hero's hopes; the princess forgets her lover and lets the ogre "save her neck"; and the hero breaks "like glass" against the "hard malice" of the villain (148).

So it is that the Daisy of Gatsby's märchen disillusions him because he is forced to deal with her as a real woman and not as a golden girl. He learns as "the knight-at-arms" learns before him, that life is unsentimental, that "belles dames" are "sans merci," and that an America of social and moral traditions is no setting for a märchen. There is much more to the story than this, of course. There is the contrast of midwestern moralism and Eastern insouciance; there is the denounciation of American materialism; there is the obvious religious overtone of the novel in which the man whose mind romped "like the mind of God" finds "what a grotesque thing a rose is." Any study of the book as a whole must treat these points.

However, we are only concerned with the fact that Fitzgerald used folklore, certainly without conscious awareness, as he went about composing his book. He may have been conscious of his debt to Keats, but surely he did not know that Keats had based his poem on a Celtic fairy motif, and his contact with and recollection of A-T 561 was probably about that of John Doe or Uncle Sam.

Nor am I the only folklorist who has seen Fitzgerald in this light. Horace Beck pursued my thoughts about Fitzgerald further and wrote the following about *The Ice Palace.*

> After your remark on *Gatsby* I have re-read *The Ice Palace* and *The Rich Boy* and would like to make some pertinent remarks about the two stories. Sally Carrol in *The Ice Palace* lives in a warm green country under a magnolia tree. She lolls around all day and listens to horns and to music. Physically she is like Mab, beautiful with dark hair and pale skin, and is young, almost immortally young. She meets the troll from the North and goes with him or is lured by him into the north country where she becomes lost in an ice palace with lights and music and almost loses her life. She even slips and spins through the corridors. Her lover fetches her to the troll king's palace with the magic wand of money. After her escape from the troll king's palace she returns to faeryland, where she lives again on milk and honey in the land of always summer.
>
> In *The Rich Boy* Anson Hunter is last seen trailing a lovely girl with a green, excuse me red, hat across the sea to a strange land hoping to find what can never be found and at the same time using the wand of money. Again in *Babylon Revisited* we have the hero trying to get back to the faeryland of yesterday equipped with money. But try as he might, the spell has been broken and he can never regain that place nor the little child he so wants.
>
> Again in a story called *Absolution* the priest has fallen under the faery spell. It is warm and the green grass is all around. Outside in the warm moonlit night the lovely blond girls whisper on the walks and he is fair moonstruck by the promise of what might be called faeryland. Take a good look. Even glance at *The Freshest Boy* and see what turns up. Maybe it stretches things but it does work.[12]

He might also have mentioned *Winter Dreams.*

Here then is a very real way in which a writer may make use of folklore filtered from the folk in creating his works. The use is integral to an understanding of the author and the works in question—and it should be studied. But it must be studied by scholars who are not preconditioned by the tidal wave of mythic and psychic half-truths that washes about our graduate schools and scholarly journals. We need scholars who will come to Fitzgerald and the rest without a compulsion for monomyths and archetypes, with minds open to the possibility that an author might borrow a technique from folklore just as he might borrow the technique of focusing a novel through Nick Carraway from Henry James. Then we will get some very fine and very needed studies. As it is now, when I start to read some more of that "myth-ritual stuff" I find an old ballad stanza rising from my subconscious,

> The first line that Sir Patrick red,
> A loud lauch lauched he;
> The next line that Sir Patrick red,
> The teir blinded his ee.

Notes

1. Erich Fromm, *The Forgotten Language* (New York, 1951), 235-41.
2. "Gatsby's Fairy Lover," *Midwest Folklore,* X (Summer 1960), 79-85.
3. See Peter A. Motteux's translation of Cervantes' *Don Quixote,* Chapter 7.
4. Richard L. Schoenwald, "F. Scott Fitzgerald as John Keats," *Boston University Studies in English,* III (1957), 12-21. The footnotes to this article contain many references to Fitzgerald's interest in Keats.
5. That Fitzgerald knew the poem well is evident not only from the Schoenwald article, but also from his references to it in *This Side of Paradise* (New York, 1920), 45 and in *The Beautiful and Damned* (New York, 1922), III, 8. In the latter, Anthony's girl, Dorothy Raycroft, is called *"la belle dame sans merci* who lived in his heart."
6. The revised 1820 text of Keats's poem is used for this article. All quotations come from this version. The ballad "Thomas Rymer" is Number 37 in Francis J. Child's *The English and Scottish Popular Ballads,* 5 vols. (Boston and New York, 1882-98). Thomas of Erceldoune,

who was frequently referred to as Thomas the Rymer, had an established reputation as a prophet and poet by 1350. Just when he lived is not known, but it was probably in the Thirteenth Century. His prophetic power supposedly came as a gift from the Queen of the Elves.

7. It would be stretching things a bit to imply that the green of the light at the end of Daisy's dock is related to the green of the Celtic Fairy. Green, which is a lucky color for the Irish, was unlucky in Scotland where Thomas of Erceldoune lived. It certainly is an unlucky color as it applies to Daisy, but that fact does not jibe with Fitzgerald's Irish background. Green, as it concerns Daisy, probably means no more than it does at any crossroads. However, it is interesting to note that the green of the fairies probably derives from their being associated with older vegetation rites. Fitzgerald uses green as a symbol of fertility and promise, and yellow as a color of sterility and despair throughout the novel.

8. F. Scott Fitzgerald, *The Great Gatsby* (New York: Scribner's Student's Edition, 1925 and 1953), 8. All other quotations from *The Great Gatsby* are from this edition.

9. Fitzgerald evidently had Father Fay in mind when he gave Daisy her maiden name. On 53, Jordan Baker refers to her aunt, Mrs. Sigourney Howard. Sigourney was Cyril Fay's middle name. The fact that Fay also means fairy and that the daisy is commonly an emblem of both fidelity and deceit may be just a coincidence; if so, it is a happy one.

10. See Fitzgerald's letter to John Jamison, April 15, 1934, quoted in Arthur Mizener, *The Far Side of Paradise* (Boston, 1951), 172. Also see his notes to Maxwell Perkins on or about April 16, 1934, preserved in the Scribner files.

11. See Antti Aarne and Stith Thompson, *The Types of the Folktale,* Folklore Fellows Communications #184 (Helsinki, 1961), where Type 561 is entitled "Aladdin" and is considered to be closely related to Type 560, "The Magic Ring."

12. Horace P. Beck to author, February 17, 1965.

The Anglo-American in Mexican Folklore[*]

The Anglo-American in Mexican Folklore[*]

Américo Paredes

There are at least three different kinds of Mexican folk groups
in the United States: the regional groups, such as those centered
in New Mexico and South Texas; the rural or semirural immigrant
groups, made up of braceros who have migrated from central
Mexico into areas not occupied by the regional groups; and the
urban groups, concentrated in cities like Los Angeles, San Antonio
and East Chicago and composed of displaced persons from the
regional areas, the more ambitious braceros, and the type of
immigrant who has abandoned Mexico either to better himself or to seek political asylum. Of these three, the rural immigrant
groups obviously are the least acculturated.

This "México de Afuera" (Mexico Outside), as Mexicans sometimes call it, is continually interacting with the parent stock in
the Mexican Republic, a condition made possible by the fact that
the regional groups are divided from Mexico only by an imaginary
line that is most easily crossed, legally or otherwise. Mexican
folklore, then, does not recognize political boundaries; not only is
there a continuing influence by Mexican oral tradition on Mexican-
American folklore but influences also may move in the opposite
direction. Nowhere is this truer than in the folklore reflecting
attitudes toward the United States. I wish to suggest that Mexican
attitudes toward the Anglo-American (or North American, as he
is more likely to be called within the political boundaries of
Mexico) tend to move from north to south, from the Mexican-
American and border areas toward the interior of Mexico.

* The greater part of the research for this paper was done in 1962-63
with the assistance of a fellowship from the John Simon Guggenheim
Foundation and a research grant from the University of Texas.

Attitudes may be expressed in every genre of folklore, with names deserving some mention even in an abbreviated treatment of the subject such as this. If one is to judge by names and epithets, little attention was paid the Anglo-American as a person in the folk-lore of central Mexico during the early days of conflict between Mexico and the United States. Even the occupation of Mexico City by Scott's forces seems to have produced no dirtier name for the invaders than "yanqui" (Yankee). Meanwhile, along the Rio Grande, where cultural conflict was a vivid and personal thing, names like "gringo" (foreigner), "patón" (bigfoot), and "gademe" (goddam) are reported by the time of the Mier Expedition.[1] "Gringo" and "patón" appear in the folklore of central Mexico near the end of the Díaz regime. Resentment in Mexico seems to have been much stronger originally against the French troops that supported Maximilian. Names like "güero" (fairhaired) and "bolillo" (French bread), now used by Mexican-Americans and northern Mexicans for the Anglo-American, originally were used in Mexico for the French. Most interesting is "gabacho," said to come from *gave,* a torrent in the Pyrenees. The name was first used by the Spanish against the troops of Napoleon I who occupied Spain during the Peninsular War; Mexicans applied the same epithet to the troops of Napoleon III supporting Maximilian in Mexico during the 1860's. In the 1930's "gabacho" reappeared, not in Mexico or Spain but among urban Mexican-Americans and applied not to Frenchmen but to Anglo-Americans. Though I questioned folklorists from Mexico about the use of "gabacho" for North American as late as the 1950's, they had not heard it so used. But in the early 1960's it began to be reported as part of the slang of Mexico City adolescents, by observers who being un-familiar with the work accepted it as newly coined.

Names are very important in revealing attitudes, as are proverbs, riddles, customs, beliefs, and particular uses made of items of material culture—to name but a few possible sources. In this paper, however, I will deal mostly with prose narrative with some consideration of song as well. Tales and songs, because of their greater complexity, are good indicators of customs, beliefs, names, and other folklore. And because they are performed in formalized situations, they correspond quite closely to audience attitudes. I will offer as part of a working hypothesis an over-simplification which I believe useful. Mexican attitudes toward Anglo-Americans from the period of the first armed clashes in the 1830's down to the present time may be seen as going through three stages clearly evident in Mexican folklore—though I do not suggest that each of these stages is strictly confined to a definite historical period. First there is an attitude of open hostility principally expressed in song and legend, especially in the *corrido*. Next there is an attitude of veiled—often thinly veiled—hostility, principally expressed in an escapist type of jest featuring dream situations in which the Mexican bests the Anglo-American. Finally there is an attitude of self-satire, principally expressed in jests which are at best mildly masochistic and at worst frankly self-degrading.

Open hostility toward the Anglo-American is most clearly expressed in the heroic *corrido,* in the legend which often accompanies it, and to a lesser degree in other songs and tales criticizing American customs. In the *corrido* the American is The Enemy, seen in the heroic terms. He may have his faults but he is a formidable foe and rarely is ridiculous. Faceless and nameless, he is more of an idea than a man; when he is singled out in the narrative he will be nothing more than the Major Sheriff or the Chief of the Texas Rangers, very much a stock type. The Anglo-American will run when the battle goes against him, he always attacks in large numbers; but though he is capable of cruelty and treachery he may also exhibit generosity. When not cruel and treacherous, he may be rich, fat, and soft, and addicted to a strange, almost sybaritic habit—that of the ham sandwich. A folk poet on the Mexican side of the Rio Grande satirizes a friend who has gone to live in central Texas in a series of *décimas* advising him to "sink those Mexican teeth of yours all the way down to the gums into the legs of pigs."[2] In a *corrido* Jacinto Treviño holds off a crowd of Texas Rangers while taunting them about their ham-eating habits. "Come on, you cowardly Rangers, always trying to take advantage! This isn't the same as eating white bread with slices of ham!"[3]

The legends about Villa and General Pershing stress the softness of the American soldier, who needs cots and kitchens and mosquito nets, not to mention ham and white bread, in order to fight. The Mexican guerrilla is superior because he is a tough man living on a tough diet of tortillas, jerked beef, and mesquite beans. But though he is soft, the Anglo-American wins most of the time because there are great numbers of him and because he is sly and farsighted. Consider the case of little Tomás Alba. He was a Mexican boy who showed extraordinary brilliance at an early age. But his parents were too poor to send him to school, while the Mexican government did nothing for him. Along came an American couple who realized the boy's genius, adopted him, and took him to the United States. The couple's name was Edison, and everybody has heard of the great Thomas Alva Edison.

Anglo-Americans have odd customs, according to the *corrido* legendry, such as that of giving away convicted prisoners to pretty girls at Christmastime if the girls will marry them. Rito García, Gregorio Cortez, and other *corrido* heroes are said to have got out of the penitentiary in this way. Usually, though, the hero refuses to marry an American girl because he does not want to become like the Anglo-Americans, who are ruled by their women. American men have their good points, but little can be said in favor of American women. Though it may be admitted that there are *some* good ones, the average American woman is seen as licentious and lewd. Hers is a historical immorality, as can be seen by the story about Virginia, the first Anglo-American ever to be born. In the first English colony to be established in America there were 240 men and 64 women, so the women slept with all the men in turn. This is a habit they have preserved to this day. Finally one of them, Virginia Smith, became pregnant. When asked who was the father of her child she could not tell. So when a little girl was born to her, the child was named Virginia Virginia. That is why there are two states named Virginia in the United States.[4] But this is what you could expect of people who eat ham to excess.

These are the naive prejudices of a semiheroic age, closely related to historical periods when armed conflict occurred between Mexicans and Americans and similar to the attitudes expressed toward the Moor in the Spanish *romance* and toward Scot and Englishman in English and Scottish ballads. Such feelings find expression in folklore that is monocultural and monolingual. This is especially true of the *corrido* legend, whose carriers most often have been monolingual Spanish speakers having little contact with or understanding of Anglo-American culture. The resentment expressed in the *corrido* may be enjoyed by audiences in bilingual and bicultural contexts, but such audiences usually find the naive details of the *corrido* legends amusing rather than inspiring. Neither have bilinguals shared this type of folklore with their Anglo friends, though at the present time the heroic *corrido* is enjoyed by some Anglo-Americans as a record of events safely in the past.

Fused traditions and bilingualism occur to some extent in the comic songs ridiculing American customs, such as the Anglo's tendency to be less than dominant over his women. "I have come all the way from Mexico," one of these songs says, "just to take a look at this American law that says the woman is boss."[5] Other songs, such as "Los mexicanos que hablan inglés," make macaronic fun of the Mexican immigrant or the Mexican-American who adopts Anglo speech and customs. There is also conscious borrowing of accent, dress, or gestures for satirical effect. This is more common in the comic song, of course, though it occasionally occurs in the *corrido*. A sheriff or ranger may be made to talk in broken Spanish, or his extremely white face (a sign of cowardice as well as a racial characteristic) may be ridiculed, as it is in "Gregorio Cortez": "The Americans were coming, they were whiter than a dove; such was the fear they had of Cortez and of his pistol."[6]

Unconscious borrowing is most clearly shown in the concept of the *corrido* hero as a man with his pistol in his hand. Modern American legend has made the knife a weapon of renegades, sneaks and murderers—of Mexicans, that is; but before the invention of the revolver Anglo-Americans respected a good knife fighter. Jim Bowie is a case in point; in an interesting reversal of roles Anglo-American legend shows him in his dying moments at the Alamo facing Mexican musket fire with his trusty knife in his hand. For a long time Spanish Americans continued to have high regard for the man who fought with cold steel, holding that only a coward seeks refuge behind a charge of powder and lead. Such is not the case with the *corrido* hero; he is Americanized. He has abandoned his knife and is always shown with a pistol in his competent fist. The earliest *corrido* heroes along the Texas-Mexican border already are pistol-toters, while their contemporaries in the interior of Mexico are more likely to carry muskets, Mauser rifles, or Winchester carbines. By the time of the Revolution Mexicans in and out of folklore had enthusiastically adopted the revolver, and soon after the .45 automatic. They had learned the virtues of the pistol by often being on its receiving end when it was almost exclusively an American weapon. The intermittent and ineffectual drives conducted by Mexican authorities in an effort to "depistolize" the population show how the image of the *corrido* hero has taken hold of Mexican popular imagination, as well as being witness to an early and profound influence of the United States on the culture of Mexico. And this without necessity of an OAS, a Peace Corps, or foreign-aid programs.

Psychologically, the attitudes expressed in the *corrido* and the *corrido* legend are related to the Mexican cult of manliness, which is part of the *corrido* tradition and as such is a natural and basically wholesome expression of a nascent cultural and national identity. There are analogues in the United States of early frontier times in the "ringtailed roarer" type who by virtue of his ability to whip all men, love all women, and outface all foreigners was the image of the manly and local values of his audience. Historically the types of Mexican folklore expressing open hostility toward the Anglo-American occur along the Texas-Mexican border by the 1850's in the *corridos* about Juan Nepomuceno Cortina, the first border raider. They reach their peak during the Mexican Revolution, when Mexican ideals of manliness, feelings of national identity, resentment against the United States, and the *corrido* tradition all coincide in one great climax that changes the very bases of Mexican life.

Attitudes of veiled hostility, released in pointedly derisive humor, rarely are expressed in song, being most common in a type of anecdote in which the Anglo-American plays the simpleton within a framework of slapstick or low comedy. This stage in the Mexican's attitudes may be related to situations in which open conflict no longer is possible, with the Mexican finding himself in a disadvantageous economic or social position. The dream situations of this kind of jest serve as compensation for a strong sense of frustration and inferiority which was not so keen when open conflict presupposed a possible victory for the Mexican. The pattern is a simple one with two main characters, a stupid American and a smart Mexican. Through the Mexican's guile or the American's stupidity, the Mexican gets the best of the Anglo-American and makes the Anglo look ridiculous, beats him, relieves him of his money, seduces his wife, or uses the American himself as the passive partner in sexual intercourse.

Such anecdotes have interesting parallels in some Negro folktales, particularly the "John" tales, and often they duplicate the boss-employee relationship of the Negro stories. The boss-employee type is common among the rural immigrant groups, where the Mexican laborer has been in a position little better than that of the Negro in the South. It is also noticeable that rural informants on both sides of the border show preference for the kind of ending in which the Anglo-American gets a beating. The ranchero, like all simple types, still gets a hearty laugh out of clean, wholesome violence. Furthermore, the jest with a beating as its resolution may be told by women and children as well as by men. Its adaptability to mixed-group telling is a factor among rural groups where storytelling still is a kind of family entertainment.

The Stupid American jest is given a somewhat different twist among the regional groups. The Anglo plays the newcomer to the region, the tenderfoot. The tales, told mostly in all-male groups, rarely end with the beating of the American, who is more likely to lose face, money, or wife if he is not used sexually himself. Similar variants are common in urban lore and among the folk groups in northern Mexico that are complimentary to the Mexican-American regional groups. As this type of jest moves into the interior of Mexico, the boss or the tenderfoot is replaced by that international image of the United States, the American tourists. Stupid American tales very much like those of the regional groups are told in Mexico City, with the gullible tourists in the title role. And in this case perhaps, the jests are less of a dreamlike character and correspond more closely to the actual facts of life.

Stupid American tales are bilingual and bicultural, though rarely shared with Anglo-American friends. Sometimes the American is just a fool, as when he pays ten thousand dollars for a burro that is supposed to tell the time whenever you heft his testicles. More often the American's undoing depends on a bilingual pun or on his misinterpretation of something said in Spanish, or he may be the victim of a custom which is different in Mexican and American cultures. An American who is working nights is told by his Mexican coworkers that if he goes by his house unannounced he will find "Juan Sánchez" in bed with his wife. "Juan Sánchez" is a common term for a married woman's lover or kept man, a variation on an earlier name, "sancho." The American hurries home, and sure enough; he runs into a Mexican who is leaving by the back door in a half-dressed state. "Stop!" cries the American, pointing a pistol at the man. "Is your name Juan Sánchez?"

"No," says the Mexican. "I'm Joe García."

"Okay," says the Stupid American, "you can go. But wait till I catch up with that Juan Sánchez!"

Mexicans are accustomed to say "It is yours" when something belonging to them is admired. This is simply a conventional way of saying "Thank you," with no more real meaning than the "How are you?" of the Anglo-American. It is a convention that has tripped up many an American, who then has complained of Mexican insincerity. The Stupid American jest makes use of this confusion. In a typical version an American and his wife are out hunting with a Mexican guide. When the American admires the guide's knife, the Mexican ceremoniously cleans it and offers it to the American, who accepts it. That night the American's wife is squatting some distance from the campfire, relieving herself, and the Mexican admires her buttocks shining white in the moonlight. So the American gives the Mexican his wife. In some versions the American is not cuckolded; he is just made ridiculous when the tables are turned on him, hastily returning the Mexican's gift when the Mexican expresses admiration for his wife, or for the American's own buttocks. The jest was told about the late President Kennedy, who accepts a wrist watch from Mexican President López Mateos during the visit made to Mexico by the Kennedys. Kennedy returns the watch when López Mateos expresses his great admiration for Mrs. Kennedy.

Conscious borrowing is more pronounced in this type of jest than in the folklore expressing open hostility, as in the deliberate reversal of Anglo-American attitudes in jests of the "It is yours" type. Unconscious borrowing also is more in evidence, especially in the acceptance of American values at the same time that the American himself is rejected. Though he is seen as dollar-crazy, the American is tricked out of his dollars. In some story variants there is even a verbal footnote in which it is explained that the tourist is paying for Texas, California, and other areas taken from Mexico by the United States.

The American woman is seen as an object both of rejection and of desire. Folk belief paints her as an insipid sexual partner compared to the Mexican woman, and as physically incapable of providing proper sexual satisfaction to a man. In spite of the Mexican's scorn she offers herself to him at every opportunity. Yet the whole point of a jest may be the Mexican's possession of the American woman as a sign of victory over the American man.

Both the dollar and the American woman obviously are symbols of power and status, and their acquisition by the Mexican in the jests is without a doubt a convenient release of aggressive feelings. Aggression is even more evident in the stories that end with the victorious Mexican making sexual use not of the American's wife but of the American himself. The symbolic use of sodomy in Mexican folklore, especially in the wordplay known as the *albur*, has been the object of much comment by Mexican writers making more or less agonized appraisals of their own national character. Samual Ramos started it all back in 1934, and the chorus was taken up by many others, from the psychologist to the poet.[7]

Consensus has it that the Mexican's use of sex as aggression is a disease peculiarly his, for which we must blame an exaggerated cult of the male commonly called *machismo*. With uncompromising Freudian logic *machismo* has been traced to oedipal conflicts arising at the moment when the first Spaniard threw the first Indian woman to the ground and raped her, thus laying the foundations of modern Mexico. Because of this primal act of sexual violence the Mexican sees sex as aggression, and assuming the role of the hated Spanish father he translates his fixation into sadism toward women and symbolic threats of sodomy toward other males. So *mestizaje*—the cross-breeding of Spanish and Indian—becomes the culprit, the underlying reason for the Mexican's spiritual ills. Expressed by a poet like Octavio Paz this can sound like something out of William Faulkner, curse of miscegenation and all.

Like all home-grown critics, Mexican censurers of the Mexican character have overstated their case. The metaphorical equation of sex and violence—the penis as sword or lance, for example—is as old as warfare. Just as old is the warrior's taunt in which he claims that he has used his enemy as passive partner in sexual intercourse. Sinfjotli's taunt to Granmar in the *Volsunga Saga,* for example, could well be envied by any Mexican *alburista*.[8] Strength and pugnacity have always been associated with virility. An Eskimo hunter quoted by C. M. Bowra boasts of being a bigger *macho* than the bear he killed.[9] In our romantic tales the hero earns the right to possess the heroine by doing violence to assorted monsters and to other males, since only the *macho* deserves the fair.

Nor is *machismo* absent from Anglo-American attitudes to anyone who cares to take a close look. The frontier cult of the male was expressed not only in the tall tale and the boast but in the Ugly Man tradition, described by John Q. Anderson in a recent article.[10] Not only is the Ugliest Man juxtaposed to the Prettiest Girl but his virile character is symbolized by the horn-handled knife which is his badge of office, while one legendary Ugly Man is named Hornbeck. The Mexican *macho* traditionally is *feo, fuerte y formal*—ugly, strong and dependable (*i.e.,* dependable in a fight). The jingoistic times of the turn of the century are epitomized by Theodore Roosevelt, who practiced the cult of manliness both in his personal life and in his foreign policy.[11] *Machismo* is present in the naturalistic writers, Frank Norris and Jack London among the early ones, though it is true that by the time the great American *machista,* Ernest Hemingway, appears on the scene the fashion has lost ground in this country. Hemingway is forced to look to other countries for settings and characters to develop his theme, chiefly to Spain and Spanish America. On the popular level, though, the cult of manliness is far from dead in the United States, as Mike Hammer and James Bond would attest.

In sum, the cult of manliness is not peculiar to the Mexican, nor does the Freudian interpretation of the Conquest explain very much. We can find all the elements of Mexican *machismo* among peoples whose ancestral mothers were never raped by Spanish conquistadors. Yet we cannot deny that in Mexican culture these elements are put together in their own special way. *Machismo* everywhere is characterized by an aggressive attitude behind which there lurks a feeling of defensiveness and insufficiency. The "ringtailed roarer" of a United States still groping for national identity is extremely proud of himself and his own, but in his xenophobia one can detect a feeling of inferiority toward the eastern seaboard and Europe. Behind Teddy Roosevelt's flamboyant pursuit of the strenuous life there is a note of self-doubt as to his ability to measure up to it. And Hemingway's hardboiled prose concealed an extremely sentimental heart. This is the same tendency, highly exaggerated, that distinguishes both Mexican *machismo* and the Mexican folklore which expresses it, especially the *albur* and the jest. Their really distinguishing feature is not the aggressive use of sexual metaphor but the careful avoidance of all female symbols or metaphors in reference to the speaker, for fear they may bring aggression directed at him.

The Mexican boy learns that nicknames and taunts are more safely put in the feminine. If he wishes to insult another boy by calling him "The Pig," he will say, "La Marrana." Should he be foolish enough to say, "El Marrano," the other boy may answer, "Yes, I'm the he-pig and you are the female," turning the insult against him. It is true that to the Mexican many words signifying coition also mean destruction, wounding, or humiliation; but the American has similar terms, the World War II SNAFU being a well-known example. The American, however, may refer to someone who nags or pesters him as "being on his ass," without fear of being the target of ridicule or humiliation. On the contrary, many would take this as a manly way of speaking. Such an expression would be unthinkable to the Mexican, who will say that someone is "irritating his penis." He must avoid all reference to his own buttocks or rectum since this will put him in a vulnerable position, open to insult and ridicule. The most popular obscene poem in Mexican tradition, corresponding to the "Diary of a French Stenographer" in the United States, is "El Ánima de Sayula," about a poor man who is raped by a ghost and passes the rest of his life with a protective hand on his backside and his back toward the wall, his other hand holding a knife threateningly before him.

This attitude of truculent defensiveness—the Mexican's well-known mistrust (desconfianza)—is the basis of his machismo and the dominant feeling behind the veiled hostility of the Stupid American jest. As a symptom of a contemporary malaise, it owes more to the ever-present image of the Anglo-American than to the racial memory of the conquistador. The proponents of the Spanish father-image thesis have had to project contemporary data centuries into the past, with no real proof that the same conditions existed during colonial days, or even in Diaz's time. The cult of manliness in the grotesquely exaggerated form known as Mexican machismo seems to be a recent development, an ingrowing of the Revolutionary code. It is a reaction to the inescapable presence of the American and his culture, a culture which at once repels and fascinates the Mexican and which is a very real threat to his awakened sense of national identity. It is due to a kind of cross-breeding, but a cultural rather than a racial one, being the congenital disease of the new middle class, which develops along with the Revolution and which still is striving, self-conscious and insecure. That is why the Mexican middle class always looks suspiciously to the north, why it often looks upon the Mexican-American and the bracero returned from the United States as cultural Typhoid Marys who may contaminate it.

But the Mexican, alas, has been looking in the wrong direction all these years; the primary base for dissemination of United States influences has become Mexico City itself. The Mexican may seek escape by going to "charro" movies, only to find that the basic Mexican symbols have become Hollywoodized. If he turns on the TV he will watch Mexican imitations of Elvis Presley, the Beatles, and Jackie Gleason. And if he takes a walk along any busy city street, he may enjoy the spectacle of Indian girls with their hair bleached a strawy blond, so sadly reminiscent of the American Negro's attempt to straighten out his hair. Thus the Mexican, on guard against the United States, finds that while he has been facing north in a posture of defense he has been outflanked and taken from behind.

It would appear that the attitudes of the Mexican middle class in regard to Anglo-American culture no longer are radically different from those of the Mexican-American, in spite of the fact that to the Mexican the very existence of the Mexican-American may be another cause for resentment against the United States. But the Mexican-American also is a living dilemma. The same strong sense of national identity, interpreted in personal terms, makes him try at all costs to preserve his Mexican self even as he yields to the irresistible demands of the majority culture which surrounds him. One way out for both is the thinly veiled hostility of *machismo* and the Stupid American jest. Another way is the satire of the self-directed anecdote, although this third stage in Mexican attitudes toward the Anglo-American may be expressed in other forms of folklore such as bilingual songs, proverbial expressions, and epithets. At its best the self-directed anecdote is a vehicle for wisdom and insight into the Mexican's predicament vis-à-vis the American, a mechanism which helps him accept the world as it is. Two *compadres* in Mexico are discussing the United States and the sensitive question of Mexican territory lost to the United States.

"These Gringos are terrible people," says one. "Cheaters, liars and robbers."

"Sure, *compadre*," says the other, "Look what they did in '46. They took half our national territory."

"Yes, *compadre*," says the first, "and the half with all the paved roads."

Fully to appreciate the satire it is necessary to know that the phrase "half our national territory" has been a common one with Mexican orators denouncing American manifest destiny. In Texas the two *compadres* may be found in a rundown beer joint in the Mexican section of Kingsville. All of a sudden one of them yells, "Yoo-hoo-ee, *compadre*! I think I'll just go out and sell the King Ranch!"

"Quit your fooling, *compadre*," says the other one. "You know I don't want to buy it."

The tendency among some Mexican-Americans to call themselves "Latins" or "Spanish" rather than Mexicans and the exaggerated sexuality of *machismo* are satirized in the story about the boy who in New York City was known as "The Passionate Spaniard" but who was just a fuckin Mexican back home in Texas.

Machismo is more pointedly attacked in another story about some Mexicans visiting a fancy nightclub. The cigarette girl is calling out, "Candy, chewing gum, cigarettes. Candy, chewing gum, cigarettes." But when she passes their table she says, "Bird seed, condoms, boxing gloves." A Mexican follows her and demands an explanation. "Because when you Mexicans get drunk," she says, "all you want to do is sing, fuck, and fight."

A belief taken seriously in the *corrido* legend, that Mexican ingenuity can more than compensate for North American technology, is satirized in jests where a Mexican is called in to solve in his own way a problem that has baffled the scientists or philosophers of the world. The question may be a very esoteric one, such as establishing what General Custer's last thoughts were at Little Big Horn. Stories ridiculing Mexican technology are closer to outright masochism, but they also satirize well-known foibles and vanities. There is the tale about the Japanese gun crew in World War II, urgently told by their commander not to shoot at a Mexican plane flying overhead. "It will fall down all by itself," says the Japanese officer. This again is a satire on *machismo,* the Japanese shown as apparently too scared to rile a Mexican, but it touches gently on another point, the once friendly relations between Japan and Mexico broken by Mexico's alliance with its traditional enemy, the United States. Fun is also poked at Mexico's great pride over its 201st Squadron, its only combat unit in the war.

Still other jests show little except an urge for self-degradation. Several nations compete in designing the submarine which will stay longest under water, and Mexico wins. Its submarine never comes up. Then there is the story that a Mexican named Manuel rode on a space-ship with an American astronaut. After having answered a call of nature the astronaut was heard to say, "I am now going to put it on Manuel (manual)."

Tales of this sort are of course strongly bilingual and bicultural. They are shared with the Anglo-American, who may have originated some of them himself. Conscious borrowings for comic purposes are not as pronounced as in the jest expressing veiled hostility. The Anglo-American is not always present as a character, though his influence always is implied. It is the Mexican who is now the protagonist and the ridiculous figure as well. It is the Mexican rather than the American who may be the victim of a bilingual pun or a bicultural situation. Unconscious borrowings become much more important; not only motifs but whole narratives may be taken over from American oral tradition and adapted. The "expertise" jest about Custer's last thoughts is an example. The bilingual will tell the story in Spanish, describing in that language the painting from which the Mexican in the story must interpret Custer's last thoughts and which shows an eye, a cow with a halo, and a border of Indians in the act of coitus. Then he delivers the answer, "Holy cow! Look at them fuckin Indians!" in English, making it more effective because it is more unexpected.

The self-critical jest is told in all Mexican folklore areas, but more than the *corrido* or the jest of veiled hostility it can be identified with the direct influence of United States culture. Some jests of this type are popular with Anglo-Americans, among whom they form part of a corpus of "ethnic" jokes along with stories about Negroes, Jews, or Irishmen. Many undoubtedly were evolved by Mexican-Americans, who as individuals caught between two cultures were more apt to look with a critical and ridiculing eye now at the American, now at the Mexican. Many others no doubt have originated in Mexico, in the more cosmopolitan circles, most likely during recent decades. It is my own experience that some 35 years ago this kind of jest was restricted almost entirely to Mexican-Americans, who might have imperiled life or limb by telling them on the Mexican side of the border. Now the self-critical jest is current throughout Mexico, though the Mexican prefers to tell it on himself rather than hearing it on the lips of the Anglo or the Mexican-American.

It will be seen by the most casual student of the jest that these self-directed Mexican tales show a strong resemblance to Jewish humor. There is the same ambivalent attitude toward the member of a more powerful group—Gringo or Goy—expressed in a comic framework approaching sophisticated wit. There is also the same suggestion of masochism, arising from mixed feelings of acceptance and protest, a passive protest that has not only gone beyond the possibility of violence but has even abandoned an imaginary aggressiveness as satisfactory compensation. Whatever its limitations, though, it is clear that the self-directed jest expresses much more mature and realistic attitudes than does the jest of the Stupid American type.

It is not only the Mexican who in these times faces a world that is more than man can cope with, and therein lies the appeal of the self-directed jest. We find the same thing in an American tradition of a more literary sort. In American frontier humor the protagonist resembles the Mexican hero of the jest of veiled hostility: the Davy Crockett type who is his own main character, coarse, full of bumptiousness and xenophobia, bulling his crude way through situations in which the laugh seems to be on him but which in the end falls on the foreigner or the Eastern dude. We have seen how the Mexican folk hero goes from confidence and violence to an ineffectual state in which he realizes his insignificance in a complicated and incomprehensible world. The same thing may be seen in American humor, where Davy Crockett has become James Thurber. The Thurber humor uses the same patterns, the same devices of frontier humor, changing little except the nature of the protagonist, who no longer is crude and self-confident but has become a lonely little figure lost in the mazes of his own inadequacy. And perhaps we see here as well the hero of modern fiction contrasted with the champions of a more heroic age. We do not need to be reminded that Charles Chaplin on the screen and Charlie Brown of the "Peanuts" comic strip are but variant aspects of the same figure, or that Prufrock is a more serious equivalent of the same. Thus the Mexican works through a series of attitudes in regard to the inescapable actuality which the Anglo-American represents for him, not only moving toward greater wit and wisdom but attaining a kind of universality as well. His humor becomes part of a general *Weltansicht* rather than a cry expressing nothing more than his own particular pain.

Notes

1. See John C. Duval, *The Adventures of Bigfoot Wallace* (Philadelphia, 1871) for use of "gringo" and "patón" in 1842. For "gademe" I have only oral reports that it was used of the Americans during the Mier Expedition. "Gademe" is used mostly by older monolinguals, has almost disappeared, and to my knowledge is not current in central Mexico.

2. "Y sumir hasta el troncón/ esos dientes mexicanos/ en pierniles de marranos. . . ."

3. "Éntrenle rinches cobardes,/ validos de la ocasión,/ no van a comer pan blanco/ con tajadas de jamón."

4. Informant No. 15, 76 yrs. old, monolingual, ranchero. Collected at Matamoros, Tamaulipas, September 14, 1962. Narrative was told seriously, not as a jest. The last sentences, as transcribed from tape, are as follows: "Por eso se llama Virginia. Nace Virginia chiquita, entonces le pusieron Virginia como su nombre y como su apellido, Pos así será. Por eso hay dos Virginias. Y fue Virginia y Virginia se le quedó. Hay dos estados, de ahi viene eso."

5. "Desde México he venido/ nomás por venir a ver/ esa ley americana/ que aquí manda la mujer."

6. "Venían los americanos/ más blancos que una paloma,/ de miedo que le tenían/ a Cortez y a su pistola."

7. Among the better-known books on *machismo* are Octavio Paz, *El laberinto de la soledad* (Mexico, 1950), Santiago Ramírez, *El mexicano: Psicología de sus motivaciones* (Mexico, 2nd edition, 1959), Samuel Ramos, *El perfil del hombre y la cultura en México* (Mexico, 1934), and Leopoldo Zea, *Conciencia y posibilidad del mexicano* (Mexico, 1952).

8. "Dim belike is grown thy memory now, of how thou wert a witchwife on Varinsey, and wouldst fain have a man to thee, and chose me to that same office of all the world; and how thereafter thou were a Valkyria in Asgarth, and it well-nigh came to this, that for thy sweet sake should all men fight; and nine wolf-whelps I begat on thy body in Lowness, and was the father to them all." William Morris translation, *Volsunga Saga* (New York, 1962), 113. Granmar's answer is not as colorful, but he does accuse Sinfjotli of being a gelding.

9. "I remember the white bear. . . . It thought it was the only male here." C. M. Bowra, *Primitive Song* (New York, 1963), 122.

10. "For the Ugliest Man: An Example of Folk Humor," *Southern Folklore Quarterly*, XXVIII (1964), 199-209.

11. See for example Mody C. Boatright, "Theodore Roosevelt, Social Darwinism and the Cowboy," *Texas Quarterly* (Winter 1964), 11-20.

Some Influences of Western Civilization on North American Indian Music

Bruno Nettl

It would hardly be truthful to say that the American Indians have been completely absorbed into what has lately come to be called the mainstream of American culture. And yet there can be no question in anyone's mind that the Indians of the United States today live a completely different kind of life—with perhaps a few exceptions—from the kind of existence which they had in the period before the first contact with Western civilization. Anthropological literature contains many studies which explore the impact of Western culture on the Indians, the reasons for the selective retention of certain culture traits, and the reasons for the varying reactions to European influences. In the study of Indian music—which forms part of the recently recognized discipline or subdiscipline of ethnomusicology—there have also been explorations of the current trends of history. There is no doubt that we have only scratched the surface, and that most of what is to be known is still a mystery. Nevertheless, enough information is available to make it possible for us to present, in a sort of outline form, the kinds of effects which the meeting of Indian and Western cultures has had on the musical cultures of the Indians.

First—for anyone who is not acquainted with the basic tenets of ethnomusicology and folklore—the repertory of Indian music consists of vast numbers of usually well-defined songs which live in oral tradition, presumably always changing but governed by certain laws or rules of style which can be identified empirically, although Indians do not usually have elaborate theories of music, or professional musicians in our sense of the word. Each tribe has its own repertory which may or may not have been affected by the songs of neighboring tribes. Compared to the classics of Western music, Indian songs are generally simple; yet they have features which can be described only in sophisticated terms, they have their intriguing subtleties, and their complexities may occasionally strain the perceptive powers of the listener who is acquainted only with Western music. Moreover, they exhibit features which are completely foreign to Western musical traditions, and they must be approached, in order to be understood, on their own terms and in their own cultural context. The very strangeness of American Indian music as compared to the Western art, popular, and folk traditions may be responsible for the degree to which the Indians have retained their native styles in a culturally hostile environment.

A fate similar to that of the Indian traditions befell those of the American Negro. Allowing for all of the differences between Indian and Negro cultures and the vagaries of historical processes, it is nevertheless accepted by most students that there is a greater similarity between what could broadly be called the African Negro and the European musical styles, than there is between the Indian and the European, and that this similarity is partly responsible for the disappearance of African styles in the New World and their replacement, in the repertory of Negro communities, by essentially European music modified by selective survival of Africanisms. In contrast, Indian music seems to have undergone little direct influence at the level of the individual composition; that is, the typical Indian song which is recognizable as such seems not to have taken on many of the characteristics or the stylistic traits of Western songs.

Even so, Indian music seems to me to have undergone considerable change at various levels as a result of the "discovery" of America by Europeans. This is true whether we view music as an aggregate of individual compositions or songs, or an activity involving various kinds of participation: composing, singing, playing, listening, making instruments, thinking about music, and so on. We will concentrate here on considerations which involve the specifically musical aspects of the problem, i.e., musical style. But we must realize also that music as an activity has probably undergone a larger degree of change than musical style. The deterioration of religious beliefs, the introduction of new materials for making instruments, and the invention of recording devices are some of the reasons.

We know little of the effect which the first specific contact with the music of the whites may have had on Indians. One description, by Fray Alonso de Benavides, a New Mexico church custodian, tells of an incident in which the friars taught the Pueblo Indians to sing and play instruments. Music was used to impress a Navaho chief who visited Benavides at Santa Clara Pueblo whom Benavides was trying to convert. At appropriate times, Benavides caused the bells to peal and the trumpets and shawms to be played, which evidently pleased the chief, who had never heard such sounds.[1]

Whether this first hearing of Western music by the Navaho chief had any lasting results and effects on Navaho musical culture later on is unknown. But further contacts between Indian tribes with the whites did have at least two kinds of results. First, some effects on Indian music of direct contact with the whites; second, effects of increased contact among tribes and representatives of different culture types as North America became populated with Europeans.

The use of English words in Indian songs is one result of direct contact. When Indian songs were adapted to English words, the music retained its essentially Indian identity, but the change in the verbal text caused changes in the style of the song, or at least caused the creator of a particular word-music combination to select a particular tune which could be adapted to English words fairly easily. Willard Rhodes has found that Indian cultures vary in their acceptance of English as a language of songs, and that where English does appear, it is usually in secular songs of a fairly frivolous nature.[2] An example from the Blackfoot repertory has the English words, "If you wait for me after the dance is over I will take you home in my purchased wagon." These words are followed by vocables in the style of Blackfoot songs, which fill out the rest of the melody. Here the English words are used much as are the Blackfoot words. Only in situations in which the tribe is forgetting its language or wishes to make its songs intelligible to other tribes, is English a necessary lingua franca.

Do Indian songs with English words use tunes which also show some Western influence? A preliminary answer would have to be no, on the whole; but it is likely that those songs which use English words have also been effected by various other indirect influences, such as the impoverishment of scale and the shortening of forms.

The converse of an Indian tune with English words is the situation in which Western music is used with native Indian verbal texts. This is found mainly in Christian hymns.

Impoverishment of the repertory and of the style is evident in a few tribes, and may also be one of the direct results of contact with Western culture. Impoverishment of the repertory means that fewer songs are known by tribe and individual, and fewer songs are being composed. This kind of reduction is certainly going on. But Indians have at times been amazingly tenacious in the retention of their native songs. The man known as the "last wild Indian," Ishi, who died in 1916, and who had never lived in a complete tribal environment and spent much of his life with a very few companions, was able to sing over fifty songs after his removal to the University of California Museum of Anthropology.

Impoverishment of the style is less easy to ascertain and even to define. I use the word to indicate a shortening of forms, a decrease in the number of phrases making up a song, and in general a reduction of variety and complexity. I have noted songs which may have been impoverished in this manner among the Blackfoot. There, songs which are in the typical Plains Indian style can be collected, but they tend to be shorter than those of the Dakota, Cheyenne, and Arapaho. The words of these songs are in English or consist entirely of meaningless syllables. Moreover, a type of form used in the majority of Plains songs seems to have been modified among the Blackfoot. The typical form consists of two sections, each in turn consisting of several phrases. The two large sections are similar, but not identical; the second may be a shortened version of the first, or may be performed at a lower pitch. The "impoverished" Blackfoot songs consist of only one such section which is then repeated several times.

Too little is known of Blackfoot music before this presumed and hypothetical impoverishment took place. Consequently this process, reasonable though it may appear, cannot be accepted as established fact. But it is interesting to find that many of the songs in the pan-Indian movement based on Plains Indian style, at intertribal pow-wows for example, also exhibit Blackfoot characteristics. If indeed there is such a process as I have postulated, it can be explained as the result of lessened prestige of music among Indians, loss of the original function of the songs, loss of composition techniques, lack of a need for melodies as vehicles for functional texts, and the occasionally destructive role of oral tradition, which has been known to cut songs in half in other cultures besides the North American Indian.

One of the characteristics of at least certain older recordings of Indian music is their use of melodic intervals which do not fit into the Western musical system, that is, which could not be reproduced on the piano. The exact nature of these intervals is not a point for discussion here; but let us point out that there is nothing unnatural or primitive about them, and that many of the scales in non-Western folk and art music are at variance with those used in European art music. What is of interest here is that Indian songs, which in the aboriginal environment were not accompanied except by percussion instruments are now occasionally accompanied by melodic instruments such as the piano. This means that the singing which is being accompanied must use intervals which correspond to those of the piano. The only songs which I have heard accompanied in such fashion are Peyote songs and songs accompanying social dances of recent origin. But it seems likely that the melodies, when accompanied by piano, are changed, or at least performed with variant intervals which fit the piano's scale. Or it may be that new songs, whose intervals are very roughly those of the Western tempered scale, are being composed, while others, which use the strange-sounding (to us) intervals, are being forgotten. Which of these conditions prevails cannot be ascertained, and the answer hinges partly on a definition of the concept of song, or composition, or unit of musical creation in Indian cultures.

In either event, it is likely that of the total of melodic intervals in Indian music—if we can think of music for a moment simply as an aggregate of intervals—an increasing proportion seems to fit into the Western scheme of things. Of course most of the intervals in Indian music have probably always been of a size somewhat commensurate with Western music; thus the recent development is perhaps mainly a matter of shifting proportion. And before leaving this subject I should like to emphasize the speculative nature of the conclusions as well as the tentative nature of the evidence on which they are based. But the use of Western instruments to *accompany* Indian melodies is a concrete example of direct Western influence.

A number of scholars have stated the belief that the vocal technique and singing style of a culture, which is audible as tone color of singing, remains with a culture in an acculturational situation longer than do other elements of musical style.[3] This belief is both confirmed and negated by contrastive examples from North American Indian music. On the one hand, we know examples of Western songs sung by Indians using their traditional vocal style. A version of "On Top of Old Smoky" which appeared among a group of Apache songs was heard by a non-American ethnomusicologist. Not knowing the song, he registered amazement at the unexpected range, scale, and melodic contour of this presumably Indian tune, which seemed to him to contrast markedly with those of the other Navaho songs. On the other hand, there are also some recorded examples of Indian tunes sung with the use of Western vocal technique.

A number of dances have been introduced to Indians either directly by whites or as a result of contact with European culture. These are best viewed as part of the pan-Indian movement which we have yet to discuss. In contrast to certain other features of the pan-Indian movement, which are clearly of Indian origin but have been distributed beyond tribal or regional provenance, some dances evidently come from the whites. Among them are the Rabbit Dance and the 49 Dance. The Rabbit Dance is practiced by Plains Indians, among others, and is danced, in contrast to the older Indian dances, by couples. The songs accompanying it, however, are more or less in the old Plains Indian style.

The 49 Dance is performed mainly by Indians in Oklahoma and elsewhere who have participated much in tribal mingling and whose cultures have absorbed many intertribal elements. The 49 Dance is one of a series of social dances usually performed by teenagers. It is essentially a round dance, has special songs reserved for it at least among some tribes, and evidently dates from the 1910's. The origin and name of the dance go back to the carnivals which followed the oil workers in Oklahoma and Texas, and which were called "forty-nine" camps. Indians were either not allowed to enter, or didn't have the money. On one occasion—so the most widely accepted version of the origin story goes—a group of Indians who were refused admission decided to "have their own forty-nine dance," and they began a custom which spread rapidly to other groups in Oklahoma and elsewhere.[4] The 49 Dance illustrates the sometimes curious ways in which Western influences, direct and indirect, have mixed with native traditions to form the ingredients of present-day Indian culture.

The indirect influences of Western culture on North American Indian music are mainly manifestations of increased intertribal contact and a rapid deterioration of culture centers and culture areas. There was contact among neighboring tribes before Europeans appeared, just as there was large-scale migration, for example the move of the Athabascan-speaking Navaho and Apache south from Western Canada, and the presumed move of Arapaho and

Blackfoot west from the other Algonquin groups. By no means should we assume that Indian music has no history, that at the time of first white contact it was in a primordial state. There can be no doubt that tribal styles and repertories constantly changed as a result of the inventiveness of individuals, migrations, and contact among tribes. But this most recent group of changes has come about partly through the upheavals caused by the European invaders, even though the results may have been felt by tribes as yet unaware of the existence of whites, and in areas of musical life perhaps completely incomprehensible and unknown to the Westerner.

Before the first contact with Europeans, most North American Indian tribes seem to have had stylistically more or less homogeneous song repertories. That is, except for a few very simple song types usually associated with special functions—children's songs, game songs, lullabies, gambling songs—the songs in each tribal repertory were more or less alike. Songs learned from tribes with radically different styles seem at that time to have been absorbed. Some of the radical tribal movements of the nineteenth century seem, however, to have inspired a new wave of contacts and to have caused the emergence of heterogeneous repertories.

Let us take the Shawnee as an example. The repertory of Shawnee Indians living in Oklahoma in the 1930's, as collected by C. F. and E. W. Voegelin, indicates four separate styles, or layers.[5] The simplest and presumably oldest consists of exceedingly simple songs whose form is a single repeated phrase, or perhaps two similar melodic phrases repeated, within a scale framework of two or three tones. These songs are typically associated with children; lullabies, game songs, and songs appearing in tales. Since this style is found, according to Herzog, in many stylistic repertories, and is usually associated with the same activities, it may well antedate the other more complex and regionally differentiated styles. The largest number of songs is in a style characteristic of the songs of the Eastern Woodlands Indians, and may be assumed to be the style of all Shawnee songs (except for the simplest archaic group) before 1500. A third group of songs is in the style of the Plains Indians, characterized by gradually descending melodic contour, large range, and tension on the vocal chords. These songs accompany the Green Corn Dance, which was evidently introduced to the Shawnee within the last 100 years. Finally, there are songs used in the Peyote ceremonies of many tribes, differing greatly in style. These are characterized by rapid playing of a water-filled kettle drum and a gourd rattle, certain rhythmic peculiarities, a whining but not overly tense vocal delivery, and certain characteristic formulae.

It is evident that the last two styles came into the Shawnee repertory as an indirect result of Western culture. The settling of the East by Europeans caused the Shawnee to move about the Southeast and Midwest, and to have contact first with Plains Indians, from whom they evidently learned songs in the Plains style and the style of the Peyote cult.

The spreading of the Peyote song style—which has elements of the traditional Apache and Navaho styles as well as of the Plains style, but also some distinctive characteristics—is surely due in part to the discovery of America by Europeans. The Peyote cult is essentially one of conciliation with the whites, and it signifies the adoption by the Indians of some of the superficial aspects of Christianity, including spelling out the name of Jesus as the text of a song.

In many tribes, especially those of the Plains and the Plateau areas of the West, the Peyote cult was preceded by the introduction of the Ghost Dance. This ceremony and the religious complex of which it was a part came about as a result of the settling of the West, the killing of buffalo by the whites, and the ejection of Indians from the best land after the Civil War. Initiated by Jack Wilson, a Paiute prophet, the Ghost Dance was intended to provide supernatural aid in restoring Indians, buffaloes, and whites to a condition reflecting an earlier, better historical stage. It quickly spread to the Plains tribes, and with it came a song style which was new to the Plains but reflected the musical characteristics of the Great Basin.[6] The main ingredient of this style is the repetition of each phrase, which caused Herzog to christen it the "paired-phrase" patterns. In some of the Plains repertories today, paired-phrase songs are a small subdivision, no longer associated with the Ghost Dance but with gambling games, and stylistically quite different from the older Plains songs.

Perhaps the most obvious and possibly the last, if we can make any predictions, of the manifestations of Western influence on Indian music is the previously mentioned pan-Indian movement, described, among others, by Gertrude Kurath and James Howard. This is very evident in the various pow-wows and other intertribal gatherings east of the Rocky Mountains, involving primarily Woodlands, Plains, and Plateau tribes. At a typical pow-wow of this sort near Detroit, Indians living in Michigan, Illinois, and other states joined in a three-day event which can be described as recreational, commercial, and actively traditionalist. Some seventy Indians performed dances for a white audience, with a number of white hobbyists joining in. The dances originated in various tribes, and a few were obviously of recent origin; for example, the 49 and Rabbit Dances. But the music was essentially in the Plains style, performed by six men (one of whom was designated as chief singer) sitting around a drum and singing the cascading melodies of the Dakota and Arapaho styles, without meaningful texts, and in short and tonally simple versions. The vocal style, on the whole, was that of the Plains, characterized by high tension and rhythmic pulsations. Some of the Indians came from tribes whose earlier repertories would have consisted of songs of quite a different nature. But as a result of indirect European influence all of them regarded these songs as their own. Just as they have frequently given up tribal identity in favor of a general "Indian" identity, they have given up tribal styles in favor of a pan-Indian style based mainly on Plains singing as an alternative to giving up Indian music completely.

We see, then, that the European settling of America caused Indians to move about, establishing new contacts and adding musical styles to their repertories; and that new religious and economic values foisted upon the Indians as a result of European conquest caused religious movements and their accompanying musical styles to diffuse. Both developments tended to enrich the Indian repertories, unlike the direct influences, discussed above, which tended to impoverish them.

Notes

1. Lincoln Bunce Spiess, "Benavides and Church Music in New Mexico in the Early 17th Century," *Journal of the American Musicological Society,* XVII (1964), 144-56.

2. "Acculturation in North American Indian Music" in Sol Tax, ed., *Acculturation in the Americas* (Chicago, 1952).

3. See particularly Alan Lomax, "Folk Song Style," *American Anthropologist,* LXI (1959), 927-54.

4. Norman Feder, "Origin of the Oklahoma 49 Dance," *Ethnomusicology,* VIII (1964), 290-94.

5. See Bruno Nettl, "The Shawnee Musical Style," *Southwestern Journal of Anthropology,* IX (1953), 277-85.

6. George Herzog, "Plains Ghost Dance and Great Basin Music," *American Anthropologist,* XXXVII (1935), 403-19.

The Origin and Tradition of The Ballad of "Thomas Rhymer": A Survey

C. E. Nelson

Scholars still have not decided what to do with "Thomas Rhymer." Two Germans (Arthur Saalbach[1] and Arthur Schmidt[2]) have made extensive studies of the ballad, but their studies are incomplete. Neither was aware of two texts not published by Child. Also, and more important, both critics were committed to the classic German folk theory of ballad origin and tradition, and were convinced that "Thomas Rhymer" is the product of a natural and unconscious 500-year, traditional erosion of the medieval romance, *Thomas of Erceldoune*—the only source, beyond the ballad, of the Thomas story. Both men, nevertheless, were aware of latter-day corruption of what they call the "pure" folk tradition. As we shall see, the German mind-set, if insisted upon, precludes understanding of this particular ballad and its tradition.

American and English scholars have seldom approached "Thomas Rhymer" systematically, except insofar as they have been interested in the folklore of elfin transformation and other worldly journeys. What textual comment we find in English adds up to this: "Thomas Rhymer" is very good; but it was never a widespread ballad; it is very unusual, and it does not quite fit our idea of what a ballad is. Further, the two most significant transmitters of the text, Scott and Mrs. Brown of Falkland are suspect, and so are large parts—perhaps all—of the ballad. The ballad thus has come to be considered more literary than traditional. This is not quite the correct judgment, however: it would be better to say that the ballad is as *much* literary as it is traditional.

The "Thomas Rhymer" story was first told in a metrical romance which was probably first composed in Scotland a little before 1300 by the historical Thomas of Erceldoune, a well known professional poet and seer.[3] However, we have no manuscript containing the story dating before about 1430; and by that time, over a hundred years after Thomas' death, the original poem had been tampered with. Thomas' writing has been inserted as the first fytt of a larger three-fytt poem that was put together about 1400. The last two fytts contain contemporary political prophecies which the 1400 author sought to attach to the story of Thomas' other worldly journey and the gift, from the fairy lady, of prophecy. Attaching the prophecies to the story was a tactic used to lend the apocryphal prophecies credence; for apparently in 1400 Thomas of Erceldoune still had, as he had during his lifetime, a substantial reputation in Scotland as a true prophet. This reputation, significantly, was alive as late as 1840, when pamphlets containing prophecies attributed to him could still be found in some Scottish farm houses.[4] Besides various manuscripts of the 1400 poem, we have one mid-seventeenth century printed text.[5] This printed text, like the manuscripts, uses the "Thomas Rhymer" story merely as a vehicle for prophecy.

The ballad itself first comes into sight during the mid-eighteenth century. Before the eighteenth century there is no trace or mention of the ballad, and there is no trace of the story of the journey told independent of a series of prophecies directed at a literate audience.

There are seven versions of the ballad available to us now.[6] Five of them are recorded in Child: Child A, B, and C under (37) "Thomas Rhymer," volume I; and two appended to volume IV.[7] As for the two versions not found in Child, one is an American version found in the *Frank C. Brown Collection of North Carolina Folklore*,[8] and the other is a twentieth-century Scottish version called "Sir John Gordon" recorded in John Ord's *The Bothy Songs and Ballads of Aberdeen*.[9] Although these versions do not seem at first reading to have much in common beyond the basic story, when they are compared in terms of idiom, the texts fall into two remarkably distinct families or groups. That is, great differences in language and narrative notwithstanding, idiomatic analysis reveals that two important patterns, two distinct ways of saying the same things, are visible in the texts; each version contains one or the other pattern, and none contains both. Thus there are (1) two distinct families of versions; and (2) a definitive sameness of diction among the ballad versions within each group. The first group, which will be called the Brown Group contains Child A and C, the American version, and "Sir John Gordon." The second group which will be called the Greenwood group contains Child B, and the two texts appended to Child's volume IV.[10]

As might be expected, a look at the histories of each text tells us a good deal about how these two groups of ballads came to take their distinctive forms.

What follows, then, is the briefest kind of summary of the history of the seven ballad texts: first, the four versions of the Brown group. The keystone of the first group is Child A, a ballad Mrs. Brown of Falkland sent to her nephew, a friend of Jamieson and Walter Scott, in April 1800.[11] This is the most often anthologized version. Jamieson published it in 1806 in his *Popular Ballads and Songs from Tradition.* In a letter from Robert Anderson to Bishop Percy, dated December 1800, Mrs. Brown is said to have claimed that she learned all her ballads when she was a very young girl from several old women in Aberdeen, where she was born in 1747.[12] Judging from Mrs. Brown's statement about when and where she learned her ballads, we can tentatively trace "Thomas Rhymer" to the mid-eighteenth-century Aberdeen area.

The history of Child C, the other important ballad in the Brown group, is more complex. C is the only version of "Thomas Rhymer" besides A that is ever anthologized—but it is largely Mrs. Brown's ballad touched up and "improved" by Scott for his 1802 *Border Minstrelsy.* Scott half admits this, and mentions Mrs. Brown's 1802 still unpublished version in his introduction to his own text.[13] As noted by Child, 13 out of Scott's 20 stanzas exactly correspond (down to punctuation and spelling of dialect) to 13 of Mrs. Brown's stanzas. The other seven stanzas of his ballad are for the most part Scott's own, Gothic-romantic invention. Mrs. Brown's version made a more subtle contribution to the shape of Scott's ballad too: in Mrs. Brown's manuscript text, but *not* in Child's printing of her text, the two stanzas recounting Thomas' otherworldly journey do not form a single unit. Mrs. Brown places one journey stanza as her stanza 7, and the other as her stanza 15. Thus the narrative takes the structure of journey-adventure-journey, instead of the more familiar journey-journey-adventure structure of Child's emended text of A.[14] Scott, of course, followed the manuscript text's narrative structure, and thus his C version has the double journey structure which seems at first glance, but at first glance only, to be an important difference between Mrs. Brown's version (as we know it from Child) and his C version. This matter is important not only because it helps us understand the relationship between the two versions, but because it has a bearing on the history of the other two ballads in the Brown group.

The third version of "Thomas Rhymer" in the Brown group is "Sir John Gordon" found in Ord's *Bothy Songs and Ballads of Aberdeen* (1930). This ballad has much the same relationship to Scott's version as does Scott's to Mrs. Brown's A version. When Ord published it in 1930 he noted that it was collected in the Aberdeen area about 1900 by the "late Dr. Shearer, head-master, Gordon Schools, Huntly,"[15] who published it in a local newspaper. Ord also notes that "this story in verse of Sir John Gordon" is either a modern production evolved from " 'Thomas Rhymer' in *Border Minstrelsy*, or it is a genuine north-country version of that great ballad, which has been modernized by someone not long dead. . . . It is worthy of note that the late Dr. Shearer, a much-respected gentleman, printed this ballad without comment of any kind, as if he did not know of its great similarity to 'Thomas Rhymer'."

On reading this version and comparing it to Scott's, two things are evident. First, many of the individual lines and eleven whole stanzas of the total 25 of "Sir John" come directly from Scott. Second, those stanzas and lines which have no basis in Scott have little affinity with traditional, oral poetry. Further, "Sir John" has the double narrative structure, and several other things that space does not allow us to examine here, that could be derived only from Scott.

The last version that can be placed in the Brown group is the American version. It is published in the *Frank C. Brown Collection of North Carolina Folklore*. The text was "secured by Mrs. Sutton from the singing of Mrs. Becky Gordon of Cat's Head, Sugar Loaf Mountain, Henderson county,"[16] and it was collected some time between 1912 and 1944. The American version is a compressed variant of Child's emended text of Mrs. Brown's ballad, and must have been taken from some ballad anthology that printed the A text. It is apparent that the compression was accomplished by putting together 24 lines substantially unchanged from six key narrative stanzas so as to form a very short and slightly Americanized version of the "Thomas Rhymer" story. Both textual and narrative analysis make it certain that Mrs. Brown's emended single journey text was the source of this version. All four versions of the Brown group, then, are ultimately traceable to Mrs. Brown's manuscript.

The three more or less fragmentary versions of "Thomas Rhymer" that make up the second, the Greenwood group, do not have a single reciter to whom they can be traced. However, they can all be traced to a common geographical point: the area near the ancient village of Erceldoune, now called Earlston, Berwickshire, Scotland.

All three ballads in the Greenwood group are recorded in Child. Two of them were found in the papers of Scott; however, they are represented in no edition of his *Minstrelsy*. The most important ballad in this group is the version which a Mrs. Christiana Greenwood, living in London, sent to Scott in May of 1806 after reading his C version in the *Minstrelsy*. Mrs. Greenwood got the ballad, she says, from her mother who learned it about 1755 in Berwickshire, where she grew up, from a very old woman named Kirstan Scott.[17] If we assume that Kirstan Scott learned the ballad in her earlier years, we can tentatively place the ballad in Berwickshire in the first half of the eighteenth century.

The remaining two versions in the Greenwood group, a text collected by Leyden, and Child B, are fragments of varying completeness. John Leyden collected his version in Berwickshire sometime between 1790 and 1802 when he sailed for India. He gave it to Scott who had it before he published his first edition of the *Minstrelsy*. The Leyden text had a small but demonstrable influence on the version Scott published.

The last version in the second group is Child B. This is another fragmentary ballad, found in the Campbell manuscripts, concerning which Child gives the following information: "Campbell manuscripts, 1830 or earlier. 'Old Scottish Songs collected in the counties of Berwick, Roxburgh, Selkirk and Peebles.' Collector unknown. At Marchmount House, Berwickshire." Thus, though B cannot be positively said to have been collected in Berwickshire, it was certainly collected in the general area. Its date is determinably only in terms of the manuscripts as a group, i.e., 1830 or before. It complements both the Greenwood and Leyden versions in most instances, but it is the most degenerate version in the second group.

So much for the history of the texts. By now we know that the Brown family of "Thomas Rhymer" versions is basically Mrs. Brown's ballad, which is traceable to mid-eighteenth-century Aberdeen, where Mrs. Brown claimed she learned all her ballads. On the other hand, the Greenwood group is a family of independent texts that can be traced to the same geographical area: Greenwood to early eighteenth-century Berwickshire; Leyden to late eighteenth-century Berwickshire; and B to the early nineteenth century Berwickshire area. We are dealing, then, with four not seven, primary texts, and for the rest of these remarks I will put aside consideration of the Scott, the American, and the "Sir John Gordon" variants of Mrs. Brown's version, to concentrate on Child A the Greenwood Group.

All of the foregoing outline is but the groundwork for the major task that faces the student of "Thomas Rhymer"—that is, the examination of the relationship of the Brown version and the Greenwood versions to each other and to the literary analog, or rather, source of the ballad, the romance. In this respect, of all the texts we have of the ballad, Greenwood is the most important, in the purist's sense of the term, the most "traditional." This ballad is hardly known at all—to my knowledge, only Child has published it, and since he found it long after he had printed and commented on "Thomas Rhymer" in his first volume, it is buried in an appendix to Volume IV. Greenwood, even though it is not quite complete and has fewer lines than Brown, contains the fullest retelling of the "Thomas Rhymer" story as we have it in the romance. Furthermore, the language and the expression of Greenwood compares with the romance as closely as does the narrative. That is, the language always approximates the romance, and often comes very close indeed.[18]

Taking the arguments presented here into account, we may work from the following conclusions. Since Greenwood is both in good condition as a text and is closely parallel to the romance, it cannot be far from either its origin or its source. That is, Greenwood is in too good a condition and is too full of its literary source to be very old. Since Greenwood is an early to mid-eighteenth-century text, and since all three versions of the Greenwood group are basically similar and can be traced to the Berwickshire area, we can tentatively assume that a not too remote ancestor of Greenwood and the rest of its group was purposefully reduced from the romance (which, remember, was printed as late as the seventeenth century) by some person who lived in the Berwickshire area in the early eighteenth century. If this is true, a complete side-by-side comparison of the Greenwood group and the romance should furnish a good deal of circumstantial verification. Bolstering these assumptions are the facts that Thomas of Erceldoune was a traditional hero of his home area, Berwickshire, and his name, well into the nineteenth century was still current. The maker of the Greenwood original must have been interested in these things, and having a copy of the romance and living in an area that was full of ballads and ballad singers, he composed the original ballad.

This is the only probable explanation of the origin of the Greenwood versions and the closeness of Greenwood itself to the romance. In terms of these assumptions, then, the ballads of the Greenwood group have an ancestor to which they are fairly closely related. Thus it is not unlikely that if the Greenwood texts can be combined in such a way that the gaps in each can be filled by reference to the others, a fairly good image of their original can be reconstructed. This, indeed, was the climactic step of my study. To accomplish this, I used the good Greenwood text as a basis and filled it out with lines it does not have from the closely related but more fragmentary and disintegrated later versions of the Greenwood group. I then used the reconstructed "original" as a basis for an extended three-way comparison of the Greenwood group to the romance, and, crucially, to Mrs. Brown's A text. The reconstructed text reads as follows; materials interpolated from L and B are italicized.

G   I   Thomas lay on the Huntlie bank,
A spying ferlies wi his eee,
And he did spy a lady gay,
Come riding down by the lang lee.

G   II   Her steed was o the dapple grey,
And at its mane there hung bells nine;
He thought he heard that lady say,
'They gowden bells sall a' be thine.'

G   III   Her mantle was o velvet green,
And a' set round wi jewels fine;
Her hawk and hounds were at her side,
And her bugle-horn in gowd did shine.

G   IV   Thomas took aff baith cloak and cap
B   III 2   *And lootit low down on his knee*
'O save ye, save ye, fair Queen o Heavn,
And ay weel met ye save and see!'

G   V   'I'm no the Queen o Heavn, Thomas;
I never carried my head sae hee;
For I am but a lady gay,
Come out to hunt in my follee.

G   VI   'Now gin ye kiss my mouth, Thomas,
            Ye mauna miss my fair bodee;
            Then ye may een gang hame and tell
            That ye've lain wi a gay ladee.'

G   VII 'O gin I loe a lady fair
            Nae ill tales o her wad I tell,
            And it's wi thee I fain wad gae
            Tho it were een to heavn or hell.'

G   VIII 'Then harp and carp, Thomas,' she said,
            'Then harp and carp alang wi me;
            But it will be seven years and a day
            Till ye win back to yere ain countrie.'

G   IX   The lady rade, True Thomas ran,
            Untill they cam to a water wan;
            O it was night, and nae delight,
            And Thomas wade aboon the knee.

G   X   It was dark night, and nae starm-light,
            And on they waded lang days three,
             And they heard the roaring o a flood,
            And Thomas a waefou man was he.

G   XI   Then they rade on, and farther on,
            Untill they came to a garden green;
            To pu an apple he put up his hand,
            For the lack o food he was like to tyne.

G   XII 'O haud yere hand, Thomas,' she cried,
            'And let that green flourishing be;
            For it's the very fruit o hell,
            Beguiles baith man and woman o yere countrie.

B   IX   *'But I have a loaf and a soup o wine,*
            And ye shall go and dine wi me;
            And lay yer head down in my lap,
            And I will tell ye farlies three.'

G   XV   'But do you see yon road, Thomas,
            That lies out-owr yon frosty fell?
            Ill is the man yon gate may gang,
            For it leads him straight to the pit o hell.

L, 18-21   *'O see you not that road, Thomas,*
(for G   XIV) *That lies across yon lily lea?*
            Blest is the man has that road to gang,
            For it takes him to the heavens hie.

> G   XIII   'But look afore ye, True Thomas,
>   And I shall show ye ferlies three;
>   Yon is the gate leads to our land,
>   Where thou and I sae soon shall be.

> G   XVI   'Now when ye come to our court, Thomas,
>   See that a weel-learnd man ye be;
>   For they will ask ye, one and all
>   But ye maun answer nane but me.'

> G   XVII   'And when nae answer they obtain,
>   Then will they come and question me,
>   And I will answer them again
>   That I gat yere aith at the Eildon tree.

> B   XII   *It's when she cam into the hall—*
>   *I wat a weel bred man was he—*
>   *They've asked him questions one and all,*
>   *But he answered none but that fair ladie.*

> G   XVIII   'Ilka seven years, Thomas,
>   We pay our teindings unto hell,
>   And ye're sae leesome and sae strang
>   That I fear, Thomas, it will be yeresell.

> L,   33-36   *'Wherever ye gang, or wherever ye be,*
>   *Ve'se bear the tongue that can never lie.*
>   *Gin ere ye want to see me again,*
>   *Gang to the bonny banks o Farnalie.'*

The comparison (which must be reported rather than reproduced here) made clear, first, the direct and full relationship, not
just of Greenwood, but of the whole reconstructed ballad and the
romance. Second, and more dramatic, the comparison shows that
despite the real generic differences between Mrs. Brown's ballad
and the Greenwood ballads, there is a submerged structure of
sameness, idiomatic and narrative, beneath the differences. No
single one of the Greenwood ballads can be brought fully to terms
with Brown, *but the reconstructed original can be:* it is clearly
and consistently visible in the Brown ballad. No less than 30 of
Brown's 64 lines reflect the reconstructed text in such a way that
one may confidently conclude that Mrs. Brown's ballad was ultimately derived from the same archetype as was the Greenwood
ballads,[19] even though it was much modified by its journey from
Berwickshire to Aberdeen, and by the kind of "creative" ballad
singing that Bertand Bronson has shown to be characteristic of
Mrs. Brown.[20] Further, Brown cannot be a separate conscious

reduction of the romance, nor can it be a part of a separate from Berwickshire "Thomas Rhymer" tradition.

The limitations of a study of this type are clear. No completely accurate and all-inclusive analysis of traditional materials is really possible—too many variables, both recognizable and unrecognizable, are at work. Even when the student is dealing with such a limited number of documents as are dealt with here, the number of indeterminables is large, and one must base his conclusions on circumstantial evidence arising from contrasts and comparisons of texts. In effect, the student must rely on the quantity rather than the quality of the evidence. Nevertheless, the quantity of evidence seems large enough to justify the assumptions made above and the following final summary of the eighteenth-century origin and the subsequent tradition of "Thomas Rhymer."

At some time around 1700, a literate individual of antiquarian bent and who lived in Berwickshire had possession of a text of the romance of *Thomas of Erceldoune*. This person, using the romance as a model and source wrote out the archetypal "Thomas Rhymer" ballad, a ballad that used much of the language and imagery of the romance and that told the story of the romance in complete detail from beginning to end. We know this was a composed ballad rather than a ballad developed solely in tradition because the correspondence between the ballad in its reconstructed form and the romance is too precise and extensive to be otherwise. This ballad came to be sung in Berwickshire, where Thomas was still a local hero. How this could happen is not mysterious. Scholars have come to recognize that not only the so-called "Folk" but the literate and sophisticated had much to do with the life and strength of the eighteenth-century Scottish ballad. However, the ballad soon began to come apart in tradition. Nevertheless, the process of disintegration was stopped short before it had gone too far. In about 1750 the Greenwood version, at this time incomplete but still closely resembling the archetypal ballad, was removed from tradition and brought to London, where it was many years later remembered when Mrs. Greenwood read Scott's version in the *Minstrelsy*. Meanwhile, in Berwickshire the ballad continued to be sung, but by the time it was again picked out of tradition (perhaps 75-100 years after the archetypal ballad had first been composed) it had disintegrated considerably, though a blurred and fragmentary image of the primary ballad remained discernable.

At about the same time as Greenwood was taken from tradition, the ballad was somehow brought to Aberdeen where it ultimately fell into the repertoire of Mrs. Brown. She modified the text in her usual manner, and originated a second-generation "Thomas Rhymer" ballad. This younger generation turned out to be stronger than the elder: Mrs. Brown's version, artistically finished and impressive, became the source of three other ballads, the last of which appeared in the twentieth century in America. While the Berwickshire line died out about 1800, the Aberdeen line remained lusty for another century, and today still lives a comfortable pensioner's life in academic anthologies.

Notes

1. *Enstehungsgeschichte des Schottischen Volsballade T. Rymer* (diss. Halle, 1913).

2. "Die Volksballen von Tom dem Reimer," *Anglia,* LXI (1937), 193-221.

3. For a complete "life," see the *DNB.* For all the early texts and the history of the romance, as well as important comment on the ballad, see A. H. Murray, ed., *The Romance and Prophecies of Thomas of Erceldoune,* EETS, LXI (London, 1875).

4. *Ibid.*

5. William P. Albrecht, *The Loathly Lady in "Thomas of Erceldoune,"* University of New Mexico Publication in Language and Literature No. 11 (Albuquerque, 1954). This is an important textual and critical supplement to Murray.

6. Strictly, there are eight if we include the fragment embedded in the partial version of "Tam Lin" which Child appends to his volume IV, p. 458. About this fragment, Child gives the following information: "Scotch Ballads, material for *Border Minstrelsy,* No. 15. Communicated to Sc. by Major Henry Hutton, Royal Artillery, 24th Dec., 1802, as recol-

lected by his father 'and family': Letter I, No. 77.   Major Hutton intimates that stanzas 46-49 of the first edition of 'Tamlane' ('Roxburgh was my grandfather,' ff., corresponding to I 28-32) should be struck out, and his verses inserted.   But 4-12 of Hutton's stanzas belong to 'Thomas Rymer'."

However, the problems of dealing with "Thomas" are complicated enough without bringing in, at this point, the mysteries of "Tam Lin"— and the stanzas in question, though they are from "Thomas," have been heavily influenced by their "Tam Lin" context.

7. 454.

8. Newman Ivey White, ed., II (Durham, N. C., 1952), 46-47.

9. Paisley, 1930, 422-25.

10. The following table gives a much abbreviated example of the kind of idiomatic distinctions which lead to the identification of the two ballad groups.   Child A is "A"; Child C is "C"; the American version is "N"; and Ord's version is "J"—the Greenwood version is "G"; Child B is "B"; and Leyden's version is "L." The stanza and line notations are to A only:

BROWN GROUP	GREENWOOD GROUP
(1, i)	G) Thomas
A) True Thomas	B) Thomas
C) True Thomas	L) Thomas
N) True Thomas	
J) Sir John Gordon	
(2, iv)	
A) fifty . . . bells and nine	G) bells shall be thine
C) fifty . . . bells and nine	B) bells . . . should a' be mine
N) . . .	L) bells shall be thine
J) bells . . . fifty and nine	
(6, l)	
A) milk-white steed	G) steed was dapple grey
C) milk-white steed	B) horse was dapple grey
N) milk-white steed	L) horse was dapple grey
J) milk-white steed	

11. For a summary and description of the three MSS. which Mrs. Brown left to us, the Jamieson-Brown MS. sent to Robert Jamieson in 1799-1800 by Mrs. Brown's nephew, Professor Robert Scott; the William Tytler-Brown MS. sent to William Tytler by Mrs. Brown's father in 1783; and the Alexander Fraser Tytler-Brown MS., which contains our ballad, sent to Alexander Fraser Tytler, Lord Woodhouselee, in 1800, see Gavin Grieg, *Last Leaves,* ed. Alexander Kieth, Aberdeen University Study No. 100 (Aberdeen, 1925), 293-94.

12. This letter is published in J. B. Nichols, ed., *Illustrations of the Literary History of the Eighteenth Century,* VII (London, 1817-58), 89.

13. *Minstrelsy of the Scottish Border,* ed. F .T. Henderson, (New York, 1902), IV, 84.

14. Child, of course, acknowledges his emendation. Jamieson, like Scott, used the ballad in its manuscript form when he published it in 1806.

15. Ord, 422.

16. 422.

17. *The Letters of Sir Walter Scott,* ed. H. J. C. Grierson (London, 1932), I, 237-38.

18. E.g., Greenwood I, and lines 4-9 of the romance (Thornton MS.):

GREENWOOD:	ROMANCE:
Thomas lay on the Huntlie bank	By huntle bankkes. . . .
A spying ferlies wi his eie	Allonne in longynge thus als j laye,
And he did spy a lady gay	Vndyre-nethe a semely tree,
Come riding down by the lange lee.	Saw j whare a lady gaye
	Came ridand ouer a longe lee.

19. Even in the following brief example it can be noted that only when the Greenwood group's versions are combined into the reconstructed text can the two families be seen to be closely related:

RECONSTRUCTED BALLAD IV and XIII:	BROWN III, 1-2; IX, 2-3; X, 2-3:
Thomas took off baith cloak and cap	True Thomas he took off his hat,
And lootit low down on his knee	And bow'd him low down till his
'O save ye save ye, fair Queen o Heaven,	knee.
And ay weel met ye save and see.'	
'But I have a loaf and a soup o wine,	But I have a loaf here in my lap,
	Likewise a bottle of clarry wine;
And ye shall go and dine wi me;	. . . . . .
And lay yer head down in my lap,	Lay your head upon my knee
And I will show ye ferlies three.'	And I will show you ferlies three.

20. "Mrs. Brown and the Ballad," *CLF,* IV (1945), 129-40.

Some Rhythmic Aspects of the Child Ballad

Donald M. Winkelman

Concern with the spatial relationship of the ballad is not new, although most students have been cavalier in their treatment, to say the least. Charles Seeger calls for a broader view of music, a concept of space and time in his *Systematic Musicology*; J. W. Hendren writes about the relationship between ballad text, tune, and rhythm with special concern for accent; and George R. Stewart shows some signs of approaching the problem.[1] But most studies have glossed over rhythm, forgetting that, when music is mentioned, rhythm is one of the three most important elements.

One of the difficulties in generalizing about folksong is the breadth of culture and tradition embodied in the tunes and texts. A song as widely known as "Barbara Allen" encounters a multitude of musical idioms, even though, in this case, it has been more or less petrified by song books. "The Two Sisters," with its Scandinavian relations, is even harder to discuss and reminds the student of folksong to take great care before expressing his judgments.

One can, however, make certain generalizations about ballad rhythm if the writer and his audience are cognizant that each tune does not necessarily conform to a given model. A case in point is the symmetry of ballad rhythm.

Although symmetry may or may not be seen in the rhyme scheme, it is usually found to a great extent in the rhythmic structure. The rhythmic balance within a ballad tune is so constant that one may assume the existence of an unwritten Law of Symmetry for rhythms within the scope of the Child ballads. This rule states:

> The rhythmic framework of a traditional Anglo-American ballad, a Child ballad, is so established as to provide a constant balance be-

151

tween sections—phrases or semi-phrases—of a tune. Because of this balance, no phrase is so heavy or preponderant that it is not matched or equaled by another. Note values which are unusual in terms of the whole pattern or which divide a beat or beats unequally or in any way are not consistent with the majority of the tune are repeated, either exactly or approximately, so as to maintain symmetry, congruity, rhythmic parallelism, and harmony throughout the tune. The only exception to this is in the measure leading to the final cadence where there may be rhythmic elongation which is not found earlier in the tune.

Rhythmic balance is evident in "Mathie Groves," although there is a minor change in rhythmic motives by the time one has reached the final stanzas. With a few variations, the twenty stanzas—98 measures in all—contain seven motives.

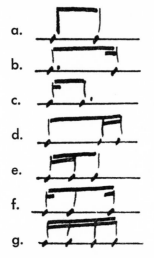

a.
b.
c.
d.
e.
f.
g.

B-c and d-e are rhythm reversals. A given pattern or motive may repeat its original form or it may appear in precisely its reverse form. At times semi- and even whole phrases may be reversed in this manner.

Of these seven motives, certain figures are obviously predominant. Pattern *a,* for example, appears 15 times, *d* is found 46 times, *c* 32 times, and *e* may be heard 26 times. While *g* and *b* are obviously less predominant—appearing 22 and 14 times respectively—they far overshadow the amphibrach motive *f* which, with variations, is found seven times, twice in a single measure. The division of these motives according to measures and stanzas points up the balance as well as showing the direction of rhythmic and their changes.

The limited number of rhythmic motives makes it relatively simple to observe their relationships in "Mathie Groves." In terms of a table of dominant rhythms, the appearance of the seven motives and their order of usage is certainly not surprising. The simple division of a beat—in this case by two eighth notes—is a usual pattern; indeed, it appears so often that no accurate count has been made of its frequency of appearance.

"Mathie Groves" is melodically and structurally the same throughout each of its 20 stanzas despite minor variations in a few stanzas. Even when these variations occur they are related to the surrounding music and do not effect the general view. Melodically, for example, there is repetition of thematic material in some 5/4 measures and most noticeably in stanza 16. Rhythmically, the stanza form is progressive and consists, for the most part, of a series of ABCD stanzas. There are a few instances where it is an individual judgment whether or not the rhythm is a variant form of another. However, there are so few problems connected with the rhythm that it does not effect the generally progressive form.

Rhythmic balance may be seen especially well by examining stanza 10 of "Mathie Groves" (see p. 154). Although the arrangement of motives makes this a typical stanza in the progressive form, ABCDD, the rhythmic elements are similar and are balanced throughout the stanza—and the song. By this stanza, the ballad is moving toward greater sense of unequal division, that is, the rhythmic elements are tending toward more dotted values and undotted fermati. This movement reaches its climax in the stanza's final seven measures. Stanza 10, however, is divided between equal and unequal division, and contains the dominant motive of two eighth notes juxtaposed with the sixteenth-dotted-eighth-note combination.

Measure 5a does not necessarily require a similar strenuously unequal element to provide symmetry since it is a ramification of the ♫. motive which has appeared four times in lines 1, 3, and 4.

Measure 3 contains a partial reversal of measure 1.

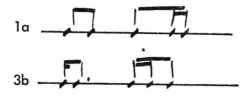

"Mathie Groves" (Child 81)

Sung by Dillard Chandler, Big Laurel, North Carolina

In this instance, the elements are misleading because of the sixteenth-dotted-eighth-note combination. However, the ♪♫ and
♫♪ sounds balance one another nevertheless and provide another
positive factor in this interesting song.

One of the most striking features of this ballad is the gradual,
barely perceived movement toward dotted values. Although this
direction is hinted at in the second and third stanzas (measures
2 and 5 respectively), it is not until stanza 7 that this pattern
becomes a more frequent feature. As noted above, this tendency
reaches a climax in the final stanzas of "Mathie Groves," where
the two eighth notes motive is constantly in juxtaposition with
dotted note motives.

Much of a feeling of ballad symmetry is the result of a reliance
upon a relatively small number of motives. As the first sheet indicates, out of 321 motives chosen from 415 variants of Child ballads,
only 49 rhythms were performed often enough to be listed, and
even here there is a great disparity between frequency of
appearance.

The problem of poetical versus musical accent is a serious one
indeed, and one which will not receive a final explanation and
elucidation in this paper. The joys of approaching the question
might be outlined in the ideas of J. W. Hendren and George W.
Boswell. Hendren suggests that the text shapes the tune; additional
words or an extra line require additional notes which are often a
repetition of the previous musical line (ABCDD). This, he says, is
a manifestation of the "dictatorial power exercised by the text
... over its musical counterpart."[2]

On the other hand, Boswell points out that the tune shapes the
text, and he cites the example of a five-line song in which the
fourth line of poetry (having three beats or accents) is too short
to fill the music. Therefore, there is a repetition of two syllables,
i.e., a single beat which leads to the fifth line. Boswell also
suggests that some texts are shortened because the tune is not
lengthy enough to provide for enough syllables.

> People cried out, heard John Henry's death,
>   Couldn't hardly say, "Him dead."
> Yesterday morning on the east-bound train
>   Came news John Henry's dead.[3]

Here, of course, Boswell is forgetting that the cultural milieu
shapes the text as well as the tune, and the informant could have
divided individual beats to provide for additional syllables. Be
that as it may, the question of text controlling tune or vice versa

is similar to the chicken/egg controversy. With that problem there may be no answer, but in the case of the domination by text or tune an answer is possible. Unfortunately, it is not possible to provide a sweeping generalization which leads the forces of folklore and ethnomusicology to joyous victory over a traditional enemy, since both Boswell and Hendren are correct. The determining factor is the singer and his tradition.

The scansion of poetic texts and the analysis of ballad tunes reveals that both have the same possible rhythmic groupings.

1 iamb
2 trochee
3 dactyl
4 anapest
5 amphibrach
6 spondee

Most important for our purposes is the recognition that studies by E. W. Scripture and others have demonstrated that the scansion structure of verse does not indicate its true rhythmic impression. In his psychological study, *Emotion and Meaning in Music,* Leonard B. Meyer observed that a great part of scansion is the mental attitude and belief patterns brought into play during the moment of perception.[4] Mursell moves in the same direction when he suggests that:

> Two persons may apprehend the rhythm of a passage of verse or music differently, and yet both may be right. What we must have in order to have rhythm at all is some definite set of expectation. . . . So long as the progressive forward-moving scheme of expectation is maintained the impression of rhythm is maintained, no matter how far the temporal regularity of the pattern is distorted.

The logical result of this statement is that there is more than one way to scan music and poetry. And as one listens to a ballad sung by various traditional singers there is no doubt that each performer envisions the metric structure in sundry forms. Moreover, rhythmical and metrical accents sometimes do, but often do not coincide. But as Boswell quite correctly points out, the music imposes its own rhythm on the text.[5] The result is a smoothness and order to the poetry which lends a continuity that might otherwise be lacking.

In a variant of "The Maid Freed From the Gallows" (Child 95) the poetic stress is usually scanned as follows:

Féy-ther, féy-ther, há yo brót me goóld?
  Há yo paíd my fée?
Or há yo comé to see me húng
  Be-ñeath tha hañgman's treé?

The music changes this, and the result is a wrenched accent.

Féy-ther, féy-ther, há yo brōt me goóld?
  Ha yo páid my fée?
Or há yo cóme to sée me húng
  Be-neáth the hángman's trée?[6]

Although wrenched accent does occur, for the most part accents are placed naturally. In any case, however, the singer seems to experience no difficulty. Perhaps this factor, along with the human tendency to speak as simply as possible, accounts for the large number of monosyllabic words in ballad texts. In any case, an example of wrenched accent appears in "Mathie Groves."

Stanza 4. It's little Robert Port was a-standing by
        Hearin' every word was said;
        If I don't die before daylight
        Lord Dan'l shall hear this news, news,
        Lord Dan'l shall hear this news.

The word "a-standin'" suggests some difficulty since the accented syllable is "stand." The notation places a first beat stress on "stan" but gives more time to the final syllable—"din."

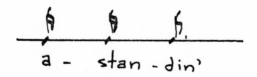

There is almost no way of pronouncing the word in speech as it must be when sung. An example of wrenched accent is in the third line of the stanza—

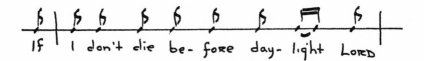

The accent on "daylight" is on the first syllable, when the word is spoken; in this case, however, both the metrical and rhythmical stresses are on "light": *Daylight*. Again, there is no problem in singing it.

Evidence thus far indicates that the rhythm and stress pattern of the sung ballad is basically the same as that of the text when spoken. As such, the regular measure distinctions drop away and a stress pattern is established based on a combination of music and text.

An interesting question arises in stanza 11 where a triplet pattern appears, but does not re-appear anywhere else in the ballad. Although this seems to violate the law of rhythmic balance, it is a necessary break, as a comparison with spoken variants reveals.

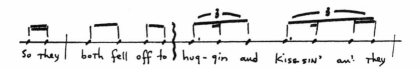

Spoken texts are basically the same:

The spoken phrases are pronounced with a rhythm surprisingly close to Dillard Chandler's rhythm when he performs the song.

At times a ballad tune contains so much repetition that it is almost impossible to miss it. "Lizie Wan" (Child 51), for example, contains a great number of similar motifs although the semi-phrases are not as closely unified as one might expect. This variant, "Fair Lucy," is reprinted and transposed in Bronson.

The rhythmic elements are related, and obviously so, although there is enough variation to provide genuine rhythmic interest.

A transcription of "Lizie Wan" points up the interrelated elements of the rhythm. Despite the loss of two half-beats (in the first and ninth measures), the rhythm is an interesting one when played without the tune, and the motives are clear and distinct in their repetition.

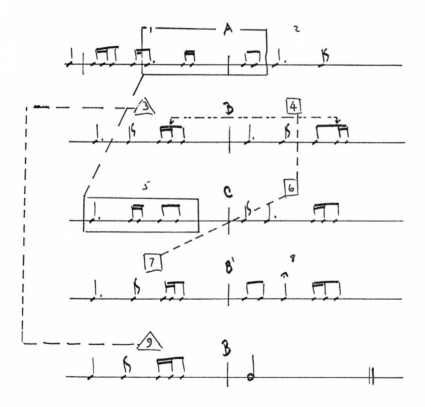

"Fair Lucy" advances by means of a dotted rhythm which may be divided into two basic motives with the hint of a possible third.

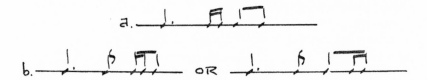

Motive *a* appears twice in fairly pure forms, although once it commences at the end of a measure rather than at the beginning.

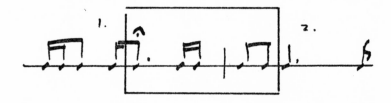

The half-beat missing from measure 1 (and measure 9) would, if added to the dotted eighth note, make this exactly the same as measure 5. Moreover, the fermatta over the dotted eighth strongly indicates that the singer was aware of the pattern.

The idea of motive *a* may be found within the structure of the song. For example, measures 6 and 7 contain this rhythm, but as part of other motives.

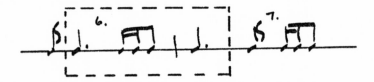

The same pattern is evident in measures 8 and 9, but commencing with the second beat of the measure.

Although there might be objections to this rhythmic analysis on the grounds that the motives are not separate entities, nevertheless the patterns are evident and must be considered as such. Moreover, rhythm is an interrelated phenomenon which crosses bar-lines with no difficulty. In this case, our mechanical system of division hinders the viewer rather than helping him to see rhythmic relationships.   Although note values may vary slightly, the basic pattern is the same, and it supports the theory of repetition and rhythmic balance which is a ballad essential.

The second motive also begins with a dotted quarter note, and this, in conjunction with the double sixteenth notes, relates this to motive *a*. There are two reversals of this pattern. The first is in measure 4, where the two sixteenths and an eighth become an eighth and two sixteenths. Here, the change is caused by the text:

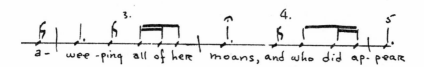

The stress is obviously on "weep," "her," "moans," "who," and, in normal speech, "[ap]pear." However, there are enough instances of rhythm which is not affected by poetic stress so that generalizations are perilous here.

Less closely related is the submotive in measure 6. Here, the first notes are in reverse order, but the dotted pattern in conjunction with two sixteenths and an eighth bear quite enough visual and, more important, aural similarity to the basic motive to establish the relationship.

The third motive is structurally weak, and consequently its elements do not appear through the tune. Moreover, this pattern is a rhythmic commonplace

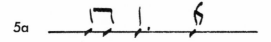

5a

which appears in many ballads. A variation on this motive uses a fermata over the quarter

5b

note which is obviously a derivative of the first pattern. In both cases, then, the dotted—or held—pattern relates these measures to the major motives of the tune.

This has been a brief introduction to a subject which generally has been overlooked by ballad scholars. As Meyer has pointed out, one of the basic problems in discussing rhythm is the determination of the "temporal limits of the psychological response to larger groupings."[7] How does one discuss rhythm and rhythmic form until there is evidence how much the average individual can perceive? And can one make valid judgments about ballad rhythm until one knows whether there is repetition because of a desire for a sense of continuity or because of an inability to comprehend varied rhythmic ideas?

The purpose of this study is a rhythmic definition, a morphology as it were, of the Child ballads. It will, it is hoped, open wide the doors for further inquiry into ballad structure and the folk process.

Notes

1. "The Meter of the Popular Ballad," *PMLA*, XL (1925), 933 ff.

2. J. W. Hendren, *A Study of Ballad Rhythm*, Princeton Study in English No. 14 (Princeton, N.J., 1936), 53.

3. George W. Boswell, "Shaping Controls of Ballad Tunes Over Their Texts," *Tennessee Folklore Society Bulletin*, XVII (1951), 13.

4. (Chicago, 1957), 11.

5. Boswell, 14.

6. Reed Smith, *South Carolina Ballads* (Cambridge, Mass., 1928), 81. Quoted in Hendren, 46, and Boswell, 13-14.

7. *Emotion and Meaning in Music*, p. 112.

A Note on Contributors

RAY B. BROWNE, associate professor of English at Purdue University, is author of over 30 articles on literature, popular culture, and folklore; editor of various books including *Critical Approaches to American Literature;* and author of the forthcoming *The Destiny that Binds: Moby Dick and After,* a study of Herman Melville.

LOUIS J. BUDD, associate professor of English at Duke University, is author of numerous articles and *Mark Twain: Social Philosopher.*

EDWIN H. CADY, Rudy Professor of English at Indiana University, is author of books on William Dean Howells, Stephen Crane, and others, and many articles.

TRISTRAM P. COFFIN is associate dean in charge of folklore at the University of Pennsylvania. He is co-author of the 4-volume edition of *Ancient Ballads Traditionally Sung in New England* and *Critics and the Ballad,* and has published many articles.

LOUIS FILLER is professor of American Civilization at Antioch College and author of *Crusade Against Slavery, 1830-60, Crusaders for American Liberalism,* and *Dictionary of American Social Reform.*

ALLEN HAYMAN, assistant professor of English at Purdue, was formerly an editor of *Accent* and is now an advisory editor of *Modern Fiction Studies.* He has published in *New England Quarterly, English Fiction in Transition,* and *Modern Fiction Studies.*

C. E. NELSON, assistant professor of English and comparative literature at Purdue, has published poetry and critical articles on Renaissance and contemporary literature.

BRUNO NETTL, professor of ethnomusicology at the University of Illinois, is author of *An Introduction to Folk Music in the United States* and many articles on ethnomusicology.

RUSSEL B. NYE, professor of English at Michigan State University, has published many articles and books including *George Bancroft: Brahmin Rebel, Fettered Freedom: Civil Liberties and Slavery, Midwestern Progressive Politics,* and *The Cultural Life of the New Nation, 1776-1830.*

AMÉRICO PAREDES, associate professor of English and folklore at the University of Texas, has written many articles and books, among them, *With his Pistol in his Hand: A Border Ballad and its Hero.*

DAVID S. SANDERS, associate professor of English at Harvey Mudd College, has written articles on Hemingway and John Dos Passos, and is author of forthcoming books on John Hersey and Dos Passos.

LEO STOLLER is associate professor of English at Wayne State University and author of *After Walden* and many articles.

DONALD M. WINKELMAN teaches English at Bowling Green University, where he is chairman of the folklore section. He edits *Abstracts of Folklore Studies* and has written over 50 articles, reviews, and papers.

This book was set in Linotype Baskerville, a face known as a transitional design bridging the gap between "old style" and "modern style" faces. The text and jacket were printed by C. E. Pauley and Co. of Indianapolis and the books bound by Heckman Bindery, North Manchester, Ind. Jacket design by Moroni St. John.

DATE DUE

APR 20 '71			
MAY 11 '78			